GOD'S
PERFECT TIMING

GOD'S
PERFECT TIMING

BREAKING THE CYCLE
OF POVERTY WITH
EDUCATION AND FAITH

DR. DAVID D. CARUTH

Foreword written by Reverend Alfonso Wyatt

WESTBOW
PRESS
A DIVISION OF THOMAS NELSON

Cover design by Tolu Onasanya

This WestBow book may be ordered through booksellers, directly from the author's website: www.davidcaruth.com, or by contacting:

WestBow Press
A Division of Thomas Nelson
1663 Liberty Drive
Bloomington, IN 47403
www.westbowpress.com
1-(866) 928-1240

ISBN: 978-1-4497-2343-9 (e)
ISBN: 978-1-4497-2344-6 (sc)
ISBN: 978-1-4497-2345-3 (hc)

Library of Congress Control Number: 2011914914

Printed in the United States of America

WestBow Press rev. date: 11/23/2011

I miss you mom

CONTENTS

Foreword By Reverend Alfonso Wyatt   ix

Preface   xi

Introduction   xiii

PART I UP FROM POVERTY   1

  Chapter 1. Active Spirituality   3

    The Caruth Family   7

    A Rude Awakening   10

    The Snow Capped Rockies of Colorado   14

    Going to Church   19

PART II SPECIAL EDUCATION AND ATHLETIC COMPETITION   23

  Chapter 2. Special Education   25

    Standing Up to the School Bully   30

    Gone Fishing   32

    My Pet Snake   33

    The Bullet Wound   34

  Chapter 3. 1968 The Turbulent Year of Change   37

    Fighting it out with my Friends   39

    The Good and the Bad in my Community   41

    Wild Pets   42

  Chapter 4. Becoming the Best Athlete at My School   45

    Tennis and the Arthur Ashe Affect   46

    Gale Sayers and Dick Butkus all Rolled-up into One   47

PART III DESPAIR AND MY TEENAGE YEARS   51

  Chapter 5. Despair   53

    Mom and Breast Cancer   54

    Abuse and the Divorce   55

    Life in Chicago   56

    Drugs, Alcohol and Puberty   59

Chapter 6. Living in the Shadow of Wealth   63
    Back on Home Turf   64
    High School   65
    1976 The Jimmy Carter Years   68
    The Summer in Boulder that Saved my Life   69

PART IV STRUCK BY LIGHTNING   73
Chapter 7. The Gate of Heaven   75
    Life after Lightning   82
    In the Belly of the Beast   84
    Life on the Five Points   88

PART V TEMPTATION AND GOD'S WAY   95
Chapter 8. Emily Griffith Opportunity School and Adult
    Education   97
    The Fashion Show   100
Chapter 9. Arizona State University with Barry Bonds and
    Friends   105
    Arizona Black Collegiate Athletes Association   112
    My First Love   121
    Salt Lake City and CLEO   123

PART VI VICTORY IN TOUGH TIMES   127
Chapter 10. The University of Wyoming and Graduate School   129
    Center for Academic Advising   135
    Campus Community   137
    From Special Ed to the Ph.D.   140
    Our Friends   142
    Fatherhood and Family Life   144
    Extended Family and the Casey Family Foster Parent Program   146

PART VII ATONEMENT AND THE MILLION MAN MARCH   149
Chapter 11. Atonement   151
    The 1995 Million Man March on Washington   153
    Fighting Back After the March   159
    The Separation of Work and Religion   161

PART VIII PASSION OF HOPE   165
Chapter 12. Earning the Doctorate   167
    African American Studies   169
    Private School for Adrian and Maya   170

Conclusion   175
References   179

FOREWORD
BY REVEREND ALFONSO WYATT

I spent my career as an educator, youth developer, advocate, counselor, role model and minister transforming the lives of countless young people caught in tumultuous life circumstances beyond their control or choosing. The aforementioned perspective allows me to understand and appreciate the profound power contained in <u>God's Perfect Timing: Breaking The Cycle of Poverty with Education and Faith</u>, by Dr. David D. Caruth. Brother Caruth unapologetically takes readers into his world and lays bare horrific childhood events namely: physical/sexual abuse, hunger, deprivation, physical, emotional challenges as well as the need for special education.

If this were not enough, David, as a promising high school football player, with dreams of turning pro, was struck by lightning while on the practice field—100 players were leveled by the bolt, David was the only one that did not get up. The story could have ended right there with yet another African American child failing to thrive, doomed to living in the now all-too-familiar clutch of poverty, crime, drugs, gangs, incarceration, nihilism and neglect—or dying too soon.

The seeds of failure were clearly sown into the life and psyche of the author. Yet the reader will discover that in the midst of seemingly insurmountable odds, David is able to change the odds. This "social miracle" was accomplished by seeds planted by David's mother, namely the seed of faith revealed in the telling of biblical stories like David and Goliath (a Divine metaphor if you will).

This young man battled a physical deformity, was tormented by siblings and bullied by neighborhood youth; however he was prescient enough to know that one day he would have to draw inspiration and guidance from the stories about God his mother taught him. Dr. David Caruth's book definitively shows how perseverance, focus, hard work, education and faith made an astounding difference in his life and in the life of his children and ostensibly, his children's children. This book shows educators, faith leaders, policy makers, parents, young people and yes, even the naysayer, how the cycle of poverty, perpetuated by low self-esteem, academic indifference, victim thinking/blaming and dysfunctional family life can be broken once and for all.

So beloved, come on the arduous and ultimately triumphant journey of David D. Caruth's lifetime. If you accept this invitation please be open to the reality that the same power that found a young boy at his most vulnerable time; the same power that snatched him from the sure grip of death; the same power that helped him overcome staggering life obstacles and receive a terminal degree, is the same power that can change the lives of readers—now that God's Perfect Timing is in full effect.

The Reverend Alfonso Wyatt has four decades of experience developing young people as well as working with public, private, community based youth serving organizations and the faith community involved in the same effort. Reverend Wyatt, a D.Min candidate at New York Theological Seminary, is an ordained Elder on the ministerial staff of The Greater Allen Cathedral of New York and he and his wife are co-authors of Soul Be Free Poems Prose Prayers.

PREFACE

God's Perfect Timing: Breaking the Cycle of Poverty with Education and Faith is about how important events in our lives happen according to God's timing, not our own. Come with me on a spiritual journey through poverty, child abuse, and my struggle to overcome dyslexia through special education. I share a chilling account of how I survived being struck by lightning at football practice at the beginning of my senior year of high school. After my dream of becoming a professional athlete got shattered, I survived on the streets with dangerous criminals.

Throughout my life, my mom, Zelna A. Caruth, was my primary source of strength. She was raised in Chicago and overcame more adversity in her life than anyone I knew. Her father died in a fire when she was 4 years old and her mother passed away when she was 12. As the oldest of four siblings, with two younger sisters and a baby brother, she called Bugs, her childhood ended at a very early age.

She was also my most important teacher and source of strength. She taught me not to criticize or judge others until I walked a mile in their moccasins. I understood her lessons, because I had seven older brothers and sisters and one younger sister, and my own shoes had cutout cardboard for bottoms. Like a sponge, I absorbed as much of my mom's wisdom as I could.

She taught me about the Bible, and to believe that God works in mysterious ways. She let me know early on in life that man would let me down, and that I needed to put my faith and trust in the Lord. If I "trusted in the Lord," she would say, and "not worry so much about what other people had," only then would I begin to see the miracles that God was performing in my own life. She was right of course. When I look at my own life, there are numerous times, too many to count, when my life could have, and probably should have ended, and God made a miracle happen to keep me going.

I also learned that not all miracles are pleasant. Unpleasant miracles are difficult for most of us to grasp. We find it difficult to understand why a loving God would not only allow, but cause unpleasant events to happen in our lives. I questioned my mom about why bad things happened to good people and good things happened to bad people. My mom's answer was that, "God allowed Jesus to die on the cross, only to raise him from the dead to glorify his own power." She left it to me to figure out the meaning of her words.

For most of us, those with children anyway, we find it difficult to imagine allowing our child to be crucified so that the world could bear witness to our power. God help us if our children get injured on fields of play. If our children get hurt, our hearts fill with pain and sadness, and we want the world to see us rush to comfort them.

We grow up learning that people who love us should protect us from unpleasant events that occur daily in our own lives. In our house, my brothers and sisters seldom felt protected. What we felt on most days was hunger, jealousy, misery, envy and multiple kinds of abuse. I wrote this book, because I believe that, in spite of the challenges we face and endure day after day, miracles happen every day of our lives; however, most of the time, we don't recognize them when we see them. After reading this book, my hope is that you will begin to see how God works through people to influence the lives of other people. You will learn how to recognize God's Perfect Timing in your own life, and to take action when the time is right. If God can bring me through poverty, child abuse and special education, back from death and homelessness, to earning a PhD, buying several homes for my family, and sending my children to private school, then you too should be able to have faith that God has a design on your life, and has already blessed you with miracle after miracle.

INTRODUCTION

The year was 1977, and I was just beginning my senior year of high school. I was seventeen years old, and my dad and I merely coexisted. He was working as a Maytag repairman and could have abandoned my little sister, Debora, and me after our mom divorced him, but he didn't. His pride forced him to work, and he did what he could to keep us from being homeless. We moved from one flea-bag motel in the red-light district of Colorado Springs to another until he managed to pay the rent on a three-bedroom apartment on the northern part of Nevada Avenue. Debbie and I were happy to have a place to live and we were glad that we could give people our address instead of telling them that we lived on North Nevada Avenue.

Our apartment complex was a huge, multi-family complex, on the outskirts of town. It was built to warehouse low income renters who were just a notch above trailer-park status. Most of the time, I walked the five miles, to and from school. Walking along the street meant walking on gravel where truckers parked their rigs, ate fast food, and solicited prostitutes. There were no sidewalks to walk on, but the view of Pikes Peak from the street was breathtakingly magnificent.

Sometimes, rather than walking along the street to school, I shortened the distance by walking across an open field and crossed Fountain Creek that ran alongside I-25. To cross the creek, I walked across a twelve-inch pipe, fifty yards long, and twenty feet above the slow-moving crystal-clear water below. Other times, I walked across the thin ice that covered the creek during the winter months. Many times, the ice caved in under my weight and I fell in, but I kept going. I ignored the freezing cold waters and the pain that I felt when my hands and feet went numb.

One particular week in August, my dad agreed to pick me up after football practice. I waited for him near the mostly vacant and dimly lit parking lot, but he never came. It was cool and dark outside, and I knew the way home. I walked down Fillmore hill, crossed I-25, and began walking down Nevada Avenue. As I passed the K-Mart and red-light district motels, I flirted with the prostitutes who propositioned me. Somehow talking to the prostitutes changed my focus from the future, to the here and now. In the here and now, I was hungry and broke, and on top of that, I was exhausted from a week of practice and working my part-time job as a dishwasher on the weekends.

As I continued along my way, I walked past the dog track where desperate gamblers tried to beat the odds. I saw my dad through the fence throwing down a handful of losing tickets. He had lots of company, and somehow, he and the other losers appeared to be delighted by their misfortune, and smiled broadly. As far as I could tell, my dad gambled all of my life, but rarely won. When I got home, there was no food in the apartment and only ice and water in the fridge. I was hungry, angry at my dad, and I prayed to God that day. I challenged God to prove to me that He really existed.

God wasn't happy with the anger and challenge in my prayer, but he answered it anyway. The next week, I got hit by the largest bolt of lightning ever to hit a person who lived to tell about it. In the book of Job, chapter 38, verse 35, God asked, "Can you make lightning appear and cause it to strike as you direct?" I was at football practice at Coronado High School when a bolt of lightning ripped through the clear blue sky and found its mark on the very patch of dirt where I stood.

My coaches later told me that the thunder that followed was so loud that it leveled all of the other players and coaches on the field. What I know for sure is, that the lightning bolt that hit me was not an accident of nature, and that God didn't allow me to accept death.

The lightning bolt hit me in the head, cracked my football helmet, entered my body through the left frontal lobe of my brain, traveled down my body right past my genitals, down my legs, and exited through both ankles. I still have the scars to prove it.

My doctors used conventional wisdom to determine that my left-brain controlled hidden talents including memory, vision, language, spelling and reading, as well as doing algebra. They believed that each talent in the left-brain is a complex network of different processes, beyond those mentioned here, but injuries in that area of the brain often resulted in serious loss of those specific talents. In other words, my doctors believed that the quality of my life was going to be severely diminished.

As I lay dead on the ground, I accepted death. For a brief moment, my spirit left my body and joined the spiritual world. While in the spiritual world, time didn't exist as we know it and I felt no pain. In death, understanding God's Will didn't happen as we experience it on a daily basis, but through instant understanding that can only be described as taking less than a nanosecond.

In a split second, I saw my own life filled with struggle and pain. I saw misery, sorrow, loneliness, and the pain that I would have to endure throughout my life. I also saw moments of unexpected joy, triumph over adversity, and happiness. I hoped against knowing, in vain, that I would not have to live that life, feel the pain of being hit by lightning, or have to live with the permanent injuries that resulted.

From the moment I got struck by lightning, God's message to me was crystal-clear and unambiguous. He was not ending my time here on earth; instead, He was letting me know that He heard my prayers and that He had the power to change my life forever.

Following my brief, but painfully real experience with death, I also experienced life in a coma. Most people don't understand what happens when a person is in a coma. My mom told me that after the doctor learned that she was a registered nurse, he told her that I was in a deep state of unconsciousness or a vegetative state. He explained that technically, I was alive. I was able to breathe and had circulation, but my brain was dead. He also told her that I appeared normal, but my cognitive abilities had ceased to function.

For four days after that fate-filled day, I laid motionless in the hospital. My heart stopped beating, a couple of times, only to be restarted by the hospital staff. Believe me when I say that there is a world of difference between being dead and living in a coma. When I woke from the coma, I had to live the life that flashed before my eyes.

I knew that God answered my prayer, and that I had to live with it. I didn't have to like it, but I had to live with it. For the first time, my conscious body felt the pain of being struck by the largest bolt of lightning ever to hit a human being who lived to tell about it.

My brother Joe, who was at the hospital for nearly four days following the lightning strike, told me that Dr. Kennedy told him that the lightning bolt that hit me knocked me straight into medical history and that I would never be same again. God changed my life that day, in the blink of an eye. Dr. Kennedy was right; I would never be the same.

As I regained consciousness in an unfamiliar room, I noticed that I was strapped down to a bed, with all sorts of tubes and wires connected to my body. The pain was excruciating. It felt like someone slammed me on the left side of my head with a sledgehammer; and while I was still conscious, yet defenseless, doused me with gasoline and set me on fire, jammed ice picks in both ears, burned my eyes, crippled my legs and damaged my brain.

When I tried to move my head from side to side to look around the room, it felt like someone had tried to cut my head off, but failed. The lightning had burned my neck, too. The gold chain that I wore around my neck, disintegrated when the lightning struck, leaving a permanent mark around my neck. I screamed, "Where the hell am I?" My scream startled the nurse, who thought I was still in a coma.

The nurse was medium height, of slight build, and dressed from head to toe in a white uniform, including a white face-mask. I began cursing, and demanding that she let me leave that high-tech room that resembled a laboratory where scientists conducted experiments on animals. She panicked, and came at me nervously, hands shaking, with a hypodermic needle full of something that I later learned would have relaxed me or put me to sleep. Her hands were shaking so much that I warned her to stay away or that I would knock her teeth out. She ignored my threat because she knew that my hands and feet were strapped down to the bed. My skin would have come off my body had I rolled over.

Much to her surprise, and to mine, I broke the strap that was holding my right arm in place. She had no way of knowing how strong I truly was. All those years of lifting weights at Nautilus Fitness Center with Crazy Joe, former Mr. Colorado, doing isometric exercises, and training in tae-kwon-do, made me stronger than I looked. With one tug, I broke the strap that restrained my right arm and landed a blow to her jaw. I didn't knock her teeth out as promised; I broke her jaw instead. She fell to the floor like a lead weight, out cold.

A doctor in the next room heard her body hit the floor, and rushed into my room to see what caused the noise. When he arrived, he saw her motionless body on the floor, and me, enraged, struggling to free my other arm. With every move I made, I felt the pain of being struck by lightning. The doctor grabbed my wrist, and tried to restrain me. But he soon learned what the unconscious nurse had learned; I was stronger than I looked. When he grabbed my wrist, I grabbed his wrist, and slung him across my bed, over my charred body, and into some of the equipment that was monitoring my vital signs, and aiding my bodily functions.

By now, I felt the full pain of being struck by lightning, and thought I was fighting for my life. The weight of the doctor's body rubbed across mine, as I pulled him across my bed. It felt like someone poured hot bacon grease all over my body, and then pulled my skin off, exposing my inner flesh to the cool air. I screamed, as I felt my skin rubbing off my body. I was hurt, angry, dazed and confused, when three more doctors and my dad, rushed into my room.

My dad was a big man, six-foot tall, and weighed over 200 lbs. He served twenty years in the U.S. Army, as an enlisted soldier, and fought in Korea before he retired from the armed service. I thought that my dad was there to help me fight off those men in white. With pain in my eyes, I reached out to him with my free arm, hoping that he would help me. Even though my Dad and I didn't get along, I was his youngest son, and thought he would help me fight off those people dressed in all white, who I thought were trying to kill me. I was wrong. Rather than helping me, as I had hoped, he grabbed my arm, with both of his powerful hands, and restrained me. He held my arm down, while one of the three doctors administered the shot that knocked me out. I gritted my teeth, and moved my head back and forth, violently, until the tranquilizer took effect. When I awoke, I found that they doubled the size of the straps that were holding me down, and I couldn't move without their permission.

Strapped to the bed, I gritted my teeth, and pulled against the restraints with all of my might. As tears streamed down my face, I screamed obscenities, and tried in vain to break the restraints. I lost my fight with the people, who I later learned, were trying to help me. Painkillers didn't stop the pain I felt, and my tears just kept flowing, like an unending stream, down both sides of my face, and into my eardrum-less ears. The drugs they gave me calmed me down, before they removed the restraints, and allowed my family to see me.

By now, I could sit up, under the beds power, not my own. My brother Joe came into the room to check on me. He was visibly upset. I could tell he had been crying because he had bags under his blood-shot red eyes, his face was drained of emotion, and he looked tired. Yet, he still tried to portray himself as an authority figure, when he told me that I had been struck by lightning. I told him, "Ya right, I'm getting out of here" and tried to walk out of the hospital. The moment my feet hit the floor, I learned that I couldn't stand, let alone walk. Had he not caught me, my first step would have landed me face-first on the floor. I had to learn to walk, all over again.

To make matters worse, I couldn't hear very well either. The lightning blew-out both my eardrums. I didn't realize that I was shouting, every time I spoke, and people who spoke to me also had to yell, so that I could hear them. My little sister Debbie came into the room to comfort me as well. I was glad to see her, and we didn't mind yelling to speak with each other. During this period of my life, Debbie and I were more than brother and sister, we were friends. She was my closest relative, and I knew that I could trust her to tell me the truth.

Debbie confirmed what Joe told me, I had indeed been struck by lightning. My coaches, Brian Beverage and Paul Hansen, saved my life. She told me that when the hospital called to tell our dad that I got struck by lightning, she answered the phone, and they told her that I wasn't expected to live. She cried happy tears when she told me the story, because the doctors were wrong. I was very much alive, but the doctors were not sure if I would ever fully recover from the injuries. She told me that I was on the news, and that and lots of people were praying for me. I believed her.

A few moments later, the nurse asked her and my brother to leave the room, so that she could remove my catheter. I am certain that both of them heard me scream, "She pulled my dick off" as the nurse removed the hose that was inserted up my penis, allowing me to urinate into a bag, while I laid unconscious in a coma. After the nurse removed the catheter, I remember saying to my mom, "How am I supposed to have children with no penis?" My mom knew that the nurse had just removed the catheter, and that my penis was still intact. She comforted me, and told me, "everything was gonna be all right." Somehow, when my mom said those words, everything was all right. I smiled, and that made her smile.

Eventually, I got used to the idea that I would have to relearn how to walk, all over again, and perhaps even learn how to communicate through American Sign Language. I also had to relearn how to read, write and do math. The physical strength that took me a lifetime to build up was gone in the blink of an eye. To add insult to injury, all I had to look forward to was going home to a barren apartment, with the man I despised most in the world, my dad.

What a week. I lost my battle over life or death with God, broke a nurses jaw, my football career was over, I could barely hear, had blurry vision, couldn't walk, parts of my brain were damaged, I had pain all over my body, including how it felt when the nurse removed the catheter from my penis. The doctors knew that I would never be the same. My injuries were so severe to the left frontal lobe of my brain, that the doctors believed that I was lucky to be alive. Believe me; luck had nothing to do with it.

PART I

UP FROM POVERTY

CHAPTER 1

ACTIVE SPIRITUALITY

I am telling you now, what no doctor can, and that is what happened to me. While I lay dead on the football field, my spirit left my body and my life flashed before my eyes. I saw the end of my life, and the day I was born at a military hospital in Fort Monmouth, New Jersey. Out of my mother's first eight pregnancies, my birth was the most difficult, taking three days of labor, and four pints of blood to deliver me. After the doctor delivered me, using forceps to clamp down on my head and pull, she noticed that I had Club Feet[1]. The doctor told her that I would grow out of it, but she had seven other children, and asked the doctor to prescribe a remedy that would straighten my feet and legs. He did. I wore braces on my feet for the first three to four years of my life.

Following my birth, our family of 10 at the time, piled into the family station wagon and moved from New Jersey to Fort Huachuca, Arizona where my younger sister Debora was born. Debbie, as we called her, was my mom's last-born daughter. I was her last-born son. In all, I had five sisters and three brothers growing up; but, Debbie and I held special places in our eleven-member family, because our mother considered us her babies. As we grew older, we learned that our true places were at the bottom of an army-style ranking system that our dad arranged by age. The older you were, the more stripes you had.

My dad, Joseph H. Caruth Sr., was a handsome man. He stood six-feet tall, weighed over 200 pounds, and had hazel blue/green eyes. His skin tone was light, but not as light as his father's.

---

1   Club Feet is a congenital deformity of the feet characterized by a misshapen or twisted, often-club like appearance.

Joseph H. Caruth Sr. United States Army

He was an only child, born and raised in the backwoods of Hopkinsville, Kentucky. His mother died at the time of his birth, and his grandmother, Lizzy Caruth, raised him. He finished sixth grade before dropping out of school, but was both literate and articulate beyond his years.

He told me, later on in life, that he resented his father, Henry Caruth, because he married the darkest woman he could find, and that his darkened skin color robbed him of his birthright. I remember my granddad. He had a very light colored complexion, straight red hair, and could have passed for being white. But he never did.

My dad told me that my granddad was a blood relative of multimillionaire William Walter Caruth, and was entitled to a share of the Caruth family fortune, which he never sought, or received. William Walter Caruth, the son of William Bar Caruth, was from Bowling Green, Kentucky. His account of the Caruth family history is titled, "The Caruth's: Dallas

Landed Gentry." [2] I don't attest to the authenticity of the information in
WW Caruth's book, especially the part where he described how black
Caruth's came into the Caruth family. However, some of the stories are
similar to stories that my granddad told me. What I do assert is that I
believe my granddad's account regarding how black Caruth's became part
of the Caruth family, but that's another story altogether.

In 1948, my dad joined the U.S. Army and served his country as an
enlisted soldier; a career that would last for twenty years. He fought in the
Korean War, won several medals including the Korean Service Medal,
with five Bronze Stars. He rose to the rank of sergeant, and retired in 1968
at Fort Carson, Colorado.

My dad's youth and upbringing did little to prepare him for raising a
large family, but he did his best to provide us with the bare necessities of life.
His upbringing, and experience as a soldier, made his transition to civilian
life as a husband and father even more difficult. It's fair to say that my dad
experimented with different ways to forge a family out of an experience that
he himself did not enjoy as a child. He was an only child, and his own father
wasn't around much. The Aunt that raised him, was mostly a drunk. In the
end, he used all the power at his disposal to control our behavior. I learned later
on in life that some of his parenting methods were both abusive and illegal.

My dad used every available means to make us fear him. In addition
to beating us on a regular basis, once I heard him brag to his friends that
he had to use everything he learned in the Army about psychological
warfare, to control his own family. I think his friends may have thought
he was joking when he said it, because he and his friends got a good laugh
out of it. But for me, he said something serious that came out sounding
humorous, because they were all under the influence of alcohol. No one
in our home was safe from abuse. Still, I loved him. At a time when there
were numerous fatherless families, at least in our neighborhood, I had a
dad, and fought for his approval and affection.

My mom, Zelna A. Wright, was a strikingly beautiful woman, five feet-
four inches tall, who grew up on the mean streets of Chicago. Her father, a
World War I veteran and coal hiker[3], died in a fire in their home when he

2   Sanders, B. (1988) The Caruth's: Dallas' Landed Gentry. Dallas: Sanders Press. Sanders
    described the Caruth's as an important part of Texas history for their role in develop-
    ing Dallas, Texas.
3   A Cole Hiker is a person who brought coal from the delivery wagon and delivered it
    to coal bins for residential and commercial customers for heating purposes.

was 38 years old. My mom was six years old at the time of his death. Her mother died eight years later, of kidney stones, when she was only 42 years old. My mother was 14 years old when her mother passed away.

Zelna A. Wright, Chicago, Illinois

Shouldering the burden of the premature deaths of both her parents, my mom told me that her life didn't get any easier. The schoolmaster asked her to leave school in 10th grade, because she became pregnant with my oldest sister Pamela. My mom was attending a Catholic school at the time, and the schoolmaster asked pregnant girls to leave school. She also had to help raise her two younger sisters, and younger brother.

By the time my parents met in 1949, she was a single mother of one and pregnant. My mom was visiting her Aunt, Lucile Wright, who lived in an apartment on the West Side of Chicago. On that same day, my dad was visiting his Uncle Jimmy, who lived across the hall from my Mom's Aunt. My mom was fifteen years old when she met my dad. My dad was seventeen years old, and had recently enlisted in the United States Army. They struck up a friendship, and my dad asked my mom if she would write to him after he shipped off to war in Korea. Two years later, in 1951, they married in Colorado Springs, Colorado.

Both of my parents were young, sexually active, and looking for someone who would accept them for who they were. My dad's decision to join the Army gave him an opportunity to escape the poverty trap in Hopkinsville, and the Army provided him with a career, that helped him provide a home for his family. My mom found a man who wanted to be her partner in life for the next twenty years of their young lives.

She went on to earn her high school diploma in 1964, and worked as a nurse's aide, from 1966 until 1971, when she was diagnosed with breast cancer. Following successful surgery, she returned to school, and later earned an Associate of Science degree with an emphasis in Nursing in 1972. Following her separation and eventual divorce from my dad, my mom supported herself and worked as a Registered Nurse for nearly 10 years before her doctor diagnosed her with Lupus in 1981.

THE CARUTH FAMILY

In all, growing up I had two parents, five sisters, and three brothers. With nine children in our family, we had three distinct groups of siblings. My two oldest sisters (half-sisters) and oldest brother made up the first group. My next two oldest sisters and second older brother sandwiched in between them, made up the middle group. While my brother directly older than me, my younger sister, and I, made up the bottom group. Our family was so large, that often times the older siblings didn't know what the younger siblings were doing, and vice versa. Being in the younger group, I had to fight for everything I got, but I was also in position to learn from their mistakes.

My oldest sisters, Pamela and Regina, we called them Pam and Genie, were not much younger than my mom, and they helped her with domestic chores. My mom and sisters cooked and cleaned, and washed dishes. I can remember them on their hands and knees, scrubbing dirt off the baseboards in our house, until they shined to a white enamel glow. They waxed the hardwood floor, scrubbed the oven until it was spotless, and did mountains of dirty laundry. My mother and sisters kept our house immaculately clean; however, underneath the well-kept appearance our house had, there was chaos, sexual abuse, tension, anxiety, jealousy, and anger, as well as fleeting moments of love.

Because of their accidents of birth, they had kitchen duty, which was more grueling than pleasurable. However, kitchen duty wasn't all bad. They seized every opportunity to eat some of the food they prepared, before it hit the kitchen table. As a result, the females in our family were healthier than the males. We were barred from the kitchen, unless it was time to eat, and spent much of our time cutting the lawn, weeding the garden, and taking out the garbage. Anyone could see that my brothers and I were not as well fed as our sisters. Our physical appearances resembled the emaciated, skeletal bodies of military prisoners, more than they did of growing young men.

My oldest brother Joseph, we called him Joe, was my father's first born child and namesake. Joe was much older than me, and always seemed to have a chip on his shoulder. He was book smart, yet naive in the ways of the street. He was small for his age and struggled to earn the respect of his friends who were much bigger, stronger and more athletically gifted than he was.

At our house, Joe was the chosen enforcer of the strict, military-style discipline that our dad drilled into him since his birth. Joe wielded the power my dad gave him to tell us what to do, without impunity. He relished in telling us who had to do what, and when, and what we could or could not eat; however, he often incurred my mom's and two older sisters' wrath. Pam and Genie took their anger at my mom and dad out on him. Most of the time, they tormented Joe for being my dad's favorite son and namesake. Physically, he was weaker than they were, and they bent his will to their own.

Joe spent much of his life trying to earn respect that never came. My mom told me that she showed Joe just as much love as she did the rest of us, and I believe her, but from what I could tell, Joe was lucky to escape with his life on more than a few occasions. One day, my mom told Joe to take out the trash, and he refused. My dad told him that he didn't have to do anything my mom said. My mom told me that she tried to hit him with a hot curling iron, but he ran out the back door, and tried to jump over the wood fence. He was short for his age, and didn't make it. She said he hit the top of the fence trying to get over, and got a huge splinter in his penis, that the doctor had to remove.

I don't think Joe ever earned the respect that he thought he deserved from my mom, his older sisters, or his friends. He didn't even have my respect after I saw him get spat on, by one of his friends, without fighting back. Most of the time, Joe beat up my older brother Richard, and forced him to lie to our mom, and say that they were fighting Mexicans. Rich and I shared a bedroom growing up, and he usually told me what really happened. I always thought Rich could beat Joe up if he fought back, but he never did.

The second group of siblings included my next older sister, Zelna, we called her Zounda, my second older brother Richard, we called him Rich, and my fourth oldest sister Barbara. Zounda was tall and darker than the rest of my dad's kids. Our paths didn't cross that often because she stayed away from home as much as she could, but when they did cross, she tried to administer her beat-downs. I was always a little too quick for her, so she relied on Rich to run me down. He did. I usually took a beat-down, sometimes I got a lick or two in, but mostly, I just called her names like "skillet," "tar-baby," or "blackie," because she had darker skin than the rest of our dad's kids. That all changed when she got pregnant with her first son.

Richard followed my sister Zounda in age and was five years older than me. Even though he was small in stature growing up, he was a good athlete, and his friends respected him. Later in life, I got bigger than him but at this time in my life, he was bigger, stronger and he had athletic gifts too. Rich could pole vault higher with a sprinkler pole, than most of the best pole-vaulters in the state, who used state-of-the-art catapults. He also could dunk a basketball when he was only 5 feet 2 inches tall. He let me hang around him most of the time, and tried to teach me things. Other than my wanting to get him back for running me down all the time, so that my older sisters could beat me up, we got along fine most of the time.

My next older sister, Barbara, was a gentle giant who stole to make sure that we had food to eat, when there was nothing to eat at home. She was a star athlete, gifted painter, and was smart as well. She could have gone to the Olympics if that was her goal, made a living selling art, or gone to an Ivy League college or university. She would fight too. If Barbara hit you, you knew it. I couldn't match her size or strength, but if she threatened to do me harm, I had a speed and quickness advantage. After she hit me, I'd get my lick in, and put some distance between us. After a while, she gave up trying to run me down, and asked our older brother Rich, to catch me for her. Many times, he did, and I suffered another beat-down.

In the youngest group of siblings, Clarence was two years older than me, and a few inches taller, but was short for his age. He also had asthma as a child, and had allergies that none of the rest of us had, as far as I could tell. One time he got a cat hair in his eye and his whole face swelled-up. He had to use medicine to make it go away. He was a good athlete too, but his sports, wrestling and tennis, were not that popular among blacks at the time.

My dad wasn't interested in his sports either, but he excelled at them. Clarence and I fought the most. When he and I shared a room, he couldn't stand the fact that I snored sometimes. One night, he got up and poured water in my ear to get me to stop. Other times I'd wake up to find him holding my nose, and cutting off my air. We fought so much that my dad made us switch rooms. He shared a room with Joe, and I shared a room with Rich.

I only had one sibling younger than me, my little sister Debbie. Unlike my brother Clarence, Debbie was tall for her age. We got into an occasional fight, but for most of our lives, we were friends. Debbie was also a gifted artist, talented athlete, and was book smart. She excelled in softball, volleyball and basketball and always kept a special place in her heart for her best friends. Debbie maintains friendships for life, and still keeps in touch with her childhood friends. We were close in age, and I usually found her friends attractive, especially Nancy and Belinda. Neither of them would go out with me, but they were pretty, so I asked them both anyway.

Academically, Barbara was probably the smartest person in our family. Some of my older brothers and sisters may dispute my opinion, and they may be right. All I know for sure is that all of them were smarter than me, I was in Special Ed.

Well, that's my family. Through it all, we loved each other. Sure we fought, called each other names, and did things to make each other's lives miserable. But at the end of the day, we were the Caruth's, and on our block, that meant something.

A RUDE AWAKENING

My first memories of life are of our home at Fort Huachuca, Arizona. We lived on an Army base, and I remember our address being 110A Fuller Street. I also remember that our Base Exchange phone number was 5685. It was hot outside most of the time.

As the baby boy, I could usually curry favor with my mom who protected me from harm as best she could. I also remember her teaching me through parables and stories from the Bible. My mom was a spiritual woman who had gone to Catholic schools as a child. She told me that she named Richard, my brother Joseph and me after Kings in the Bible, and my older brother Clarence, after her father and her uncle Frank. Her Uncle Frank took her, her two sisters and brother in after their parents died, so those names also held a special place in her heart. I always thought she named my brother Joe after my dad, because his name was Joe Jr.

I didn't know it at the time, but as I grew into adulthood, each lesson my mother taught me as a child would have a profound affect my life. She taught me to have faith, and to believe that I could achieve whatever I wanted in life, and expect it to come, not to wait for it to come, and then have faith. She taught me to shun fools, and to seek wise counsel. She taught me to read and write, as best she could. She taught me to stand up to bullies, because one day, she assured me, I would grow up to be big and strong, and that by my own hand, I would hold those that tormented me, accountable. She read me the story of David and Goliath. She made sure that I understood that, like David, God was on my side, and that I too could bring a giant down with a single blow. I smiled after learning those lessons, and my smile made her eyes light-up with pride.

When I was just a small child, no more than 2 years old, I realized that I was different from my other brothers and sisters. I was born with Club Feet. I wore orthopedic shoes, connected to each other by a metal rod. They were designed to reshape my feet and legs. With each laborious step I took, I grimaced in pain. My family and friends teased and humiliated me. I couldn't move about the house, or yard, with the freedom of normal a growing boy. My every movement was restricted, so I couldn't defend myself from pinches or slaps upside the head.

In our family, physical violence was only one of many challenges. I remember one day when my older brothers and sisters, knowing I was hungry and too young to know better, encouraged me to eat rat poison that was stored in the cabinet underneath our kitchen sink. The rat poison was pink, and looked like oatmeal. They assured me that it was strawberry flavored oatmeal. I ate it, and became violently ill. My mom was furious. She rushed me to the base hospital and had my stomach pumped. This was the first time I can remember that I escaped death. Throughout my life, I escaped death many times.

On most days, I spent much of my time in search of food, and playing. I remember one day when my brother Clarence lifted me up so that I could open our neighbor's window, which was partially open because the electrical wire to their swamp cooler ran through it. I slid the window open, crawled through it, and opened their front door. Me, Clarence, and Debbie went into their house, and stole a box of Corn Flakes from their cabinet, to stave off starvation. After all, food was a precious commodity that was always in short supply at our house. On many nights, we opened cans of K-rations, and ate whatever food we found inside. We chewed the gum, and smoked the cigarettes too. I didn't know where the K-rations came from, but we always seemed to have a couple of cases in the house.

I had a couple of friends that I can remember, Pam and Freddie. We all used to play outside in our yard, next to the four o-clock bushes. We played the usual childhood games, marbles and make-believe super heroes, but mostly we just walked around, got into mischief, and ate dirt. My mom always had to wash my face and hands when I came in from playing.

There was a drainage ditch not far our house where we tried to catch Blue-tailed Racer lizards. Sometimes I caught one, but most of the time, I was only quick enough to capture a tail, that would wiggle around without a body for a few minutes, after the lizard got away. I did manage to catch a horned toad or a "horny-toad" as we called them. It was about three inches by three inches, pink in color, and very fat. Its size made it slow and easy to catch. When I took it home to show my mom, it squirted blood from its eyes. My mom said that it was just trying to protect itself, because she thought it was going to have a baby. I put it in a shoebox, and waited several days for it to give birth, but it never did. My brother Rich saw it, and said that he heard that some people gave birth by getting their bellies cut open. He thought he could operate on my pet, and deliver its baby. He seemed sure of himself, and I agreed to let him try.

We took the toad outside, and Rich got out his army-issued pocketknife that he stole from our dad. He said that all he had to do was, cut its belly open, and take the baby toad out. Rich cut open the toad's belly, and sure enough, there was a baby toad inside. The baby was dead, and so was the momma. I ran to tell my mom. Rich tried to stop me from telling, but I was screaming so loud that she heard me. When she saw what he did, she whipped him with a broken fan belt from our swamp cooler. Boy was he mad at me, but he killed my pet, and wasn't even sorry. All he said was that he was going to be vet when he grew up, and sometimes animals died during surgery.

By the time I was 5 years old, my mom thought my legs and feet were near normal, and said, "Son, you have to move past fear, and take a step inspired by faith." I had grown used to turning my whole body, to take a step, and then turning it again, to take another. I remembered what she taught me about having faith, and believed that I could run and play with the best of them.

From that moment on, running would become both a source of pride, and a means of survival. I ran through our home with reckless abandon, and busted my head open several times. I still have the scars to prove it. Along with my newfound speed, and scarred forehead, came the taunts of "Scar-Face" or "dent-head." My brothers and sisters called me names most of my childhood. However, my mother gave me the inner strength to stand up to bullies, and God had given me a wonderful gift, the gift of speed.

My mother heard the dent-head taunts, and knew that I was smaller and weaker than my other brothers and sisters. She also knew that she taught me to stand up to bullies, which oftentimes were my own brothers and sisters. She recognized my gift of speed, and taught me that there was no shame in running away, if I stood up for myself first, and got a lick or two in. She taught me to hit and run, and get away and live to hit another day. I experimented with this idea on my older brother Clarence, and much to my surprise; it worked most of the time. The few times it didn't work, the fight was on, and I was always proud of the few good licks I got in, before I got beat up.

I recall one day, my older brothers Rich, Clarence and I went into a field near our house to eat some K-rations that we stole from our pantry. After we opened the cans and ate the food, we decided to smoke the cigarettes, and accidentally set the field on fire. We tried to stamp the fire out, but were not able to. We ran to escape the flames. Rich decided that we would tell our dad that a GI threw a grenade out of his car window, and that's what started the fire. We told our dad the story, and he didn't believe us. Instead, he beat us, one after the other, until Clarence told him that we had been smoking cigarettes and caused the fire. Clarence may have thought that telling our dad we were smoking was better than getting beat. He left out the part about the stolen K-rations. My dad appreciated his honesty, but despised him for being mentally weak, and made us smoke cigarette after cigarette, until we all got sick.

Soon, we moved from Arizona to Colorado Springs, Colorado where our dad eventually retired from military service. My mom told me that our family moved around a lot, like other military families, but all I remember is Arizona and Colorado. We eventually settled into a modest, tri-level house on 1442 N. Walnut Street. The house was new, and the basement, where all the boys slept, was unfinished. The year was 1966.

The Civil Rights era was in full bloom and people were still talking about the fact that Martin Luther King Jr. had included a reference to the "Snow Capped Rockies of Colorado" in his I Have A Dream speech three years earlier. I was surprised to learn that he knew about racism in Colorado.

THE SNOW CAPPED ROCKIES OF COLORADO

My dad was from Hopkinsville Kentucky and had experienced southern racism first hand. He made sure that his family would not have to experience overt racism, and he also wanted us to get a better education then what was available to blacks in the South.

Growing up in Colorado Springs, I always felt like my dad liked my older brothers, Joe and Rich, better than he liked Clarence and me. Perhaps he was disappointed that Clarence had asthma and other allergies or that I had been born with deformed feet. Perhaps he sensed that I was a slow learner, or maybe I challenged his authority too many times. He died before I could ask him, so I will never know for sure. Whatever the reason, he whipped me on a regular basis. Clarence told me that he thought I got more whippings than anyone else in our family. I don't know for sure, but I believed him.

Sometimes I deserved the spanking I got, but not most of the time. I got whipped plenty of times because I wet the bed. It got so bad, that I quit caring about the beatings, and did bad things to get back at him. Sometimes I let the air out of his car tires to make him late for work. Other times, I ate his favorite food when no one was looking. Usually, he got the better of me, but he never broke my spirit.

My mom was always kind to me. She came from a hard life in Chicago, but now she lived in a quiet neighborhood and had nine children of her own to raise. She was a strong woman, and taught me to be strong. No matter what I did, she taught me that there was always a lesson to learn. I learned the lessons as best I could, and armed myself to do battle in a world that she knew would take advantage of the weak.

Life at our house was war. We had to fight for everything we got, and fought we did, every day. My chief nemesis was my immediate older brother Clarence. Clarence and I fought all the time because, like all of my older brothers and sisters, he tried to assert his authority over me. When I refused to do what he said, he spent hours finding different ways to aggravate me. He made up new names to call me, and started calling me Mahatma Gandhi. I didn't know who that was, but when I asked my teacher at school, she showed me a picture of a rail-thin man who was once the Prime Minister of India. Since he was just two years older than me, I tried to stop the name-calling, and when that failed, I took my chances with fist-to-cuffs.

My dad was a soldier and made certain that we all understood how to take orders and what the consequences were for not following them. I wasn't in the Army, so I rebelled against following orders, and other form of authority. It didn't matter if orders came from my dad, or any other member of my family for that matter. In our family, I was nothing more than a two stripe private and I only out ranked my little sister Debbie who only had one imaginary stripe on her shoulder. Failing to follow orders from anyone with more stripes meant swift punishment, or more likely than not, the beat-down.

My mom, she was special. She had this strange combination of warmth, strength, violence and making sure that my brothers and sisters knew that I was special. My brothers and sisters could hurt me a little, because my mom knew that I was in a constant state of rebellion. But if they crossed that imaginary line in her mind, she would "brain" them. On a good day, she would use the coffee pot cord on their behinds. On a bad day, the coffee pot would still be on the other end of the cord. I never wanted to be them when my mom got mad. She'd pick up the closest thing she could get her hands on and go to town all up side their heads.

I took many beat-downs, fought back daily and often. My mom protected me when she could. When she couldn't, I had to choose between fighting or running or both. I followed the lessons that my mom taught me from the Bible. She taught me the story of Sampson, and how he picked up the jawbone of an ass, and slew a thousand men. If I had to pick up a stick, a rock, or even a hand full of dirt, I claimed it as my equalizer and weapon of choice, and wasted no time using it. When all else failed, I got some meters, and put as much distance as I could between me and anybody who sought to do me harm. After I stood my ground, and got a few licks in.

Outside of my genetic makeup, and running everywhere I went, my brother Clarence is probably most responsible for my speed. During the early years, he often had a strength advantage over me. To have any chance against his superior strength, I had to strike first. I always aimed for his eye or nose, or any part of his body that would leave a mark so others would see what could happen to them if they messed with me. After I got a few good licks in, I usually took a beat-down, got some meters, or both.

Oh, Clarence gave chase, often. Sometimes he caught me, and the beat-down was on. Other times, I was quick enough to get far enough ahead of him so that I could taunt him. I would run backwards and hurl insults at him. I called him "pickle-head" or "rashey-face" and just before he caught up, I'd turn and run and we both knew what that meant, no beat-down for me that day. After a while, I matched his size and strength and he gave up trying to administer street justice.

During most of my childhood, I was more interested in where the next meal was coming from than anything else. My dad had a gambling problem, and sometimes he lost his entire paycheck betting on the dogs at the local dog-track. He would come home, after losing all of his money at the track, and after having had a few drinks of Old Crow at the NCO Club on base, or the Elks off base, and tell us how close he had come to hitting the big one. That made my mom furious.

While my parents argued and fought, some of us went next door and got in our friends mother's food line. I considered Mrs. Palmer to be my second mom. She was married, and had five boys and three girls of her own. Two of her sons, Harold and Terry would become my best friends. Most of the time, she didn't mind a few extra mouths to feed around dinnertime. I was always surprised that Mrs. Palmer cooked five chickens for dinner.

At our house, dinner was the one time where we all sat around the table and shared whatever food my dad could provide. Sometimes we ate C-rations; other times, civilian food. My mom had a way of stretching even the smallest amounts of food, whatever it was. She divided a single chicken into 11 pieces, parceled out a can of peas, and made sure that we received a helping of mashed potatoes, made from potatoes she had grown in her garden. Before we gave thanks to God, and asked him to bless our meal, I counted every pea on everyone's plate, and protested vehemently if I had one pea less. Every single time, I had less, and my protests fell upon larger, hungrier ears. After losing my protests, I made sure that my little sister and I had an equal amount, usually five or six peas each. Kool-aid was usually available.

The food at our table was passed from my dad, to my mom, and down the chain until it reached me and my little sister Debbie, last. My mom split the chicken back into two pieces, and I got to chose between the booty and the back. The piece I took depended on whether the two little pieces of meat on the booty, were still in place. Most of the time, the meat would be gone, and I passed that piece along to my little sister.

I remember other times, when we ate popcorn for dinner, peanut butter and jelly sandwiches, or tripe. Whatever food we had, my mom cooked it up and that's what we ate. Sometimes she cooked fish that we caught, made gumbo, or even cornmeal mush. At our house, whatever we ate, we sat around the kitchen table and ate it together. Most of the time, when I asked to be excused from the table, I left hungry. The few times I left full, were usually around Easter, Christmas or Thanks Giving, or when bananas were on sale, and my mom made a huge bowl of banana pudding with vanilla wafers on top.

There were other times, when we sat around the kitchen table waiting for my dad to bring dinner home. After waiting for two hours or so, I asked to be excused and went next door to the Palmers. Sometimes I played with my friends until they had dinner hoping that Mrs. Palmer would invite me to have dinner with them. I think she knew that I was there at dinnertime because I was hungry, but she never made me feel bad because of it. Sometimes, it didn't work because she would hear my mom calling me and sent me home. My brother Rich told me that sometimes the older kids waited-up until midnight, and my dad would bring home hamburgers after the younger kids went to bed hungry.

I used to say that our family was "po" because we couldn't to afford the other "o" and the "r" that would have made us poor like the other families in our neighborhood. It got so bad sometimes, that we ate the cartilage right off the bone, broke the chicken bones open, and sucked the bone marrow out. My starving dog, Sampson, often buried those bones for a day when he couldn't escape his leash and knock over a trash can or two down the alley.

The worst part of not getting enough to eat at our house was when my dad ate lobster and crab legs in front of us. I wanted to ask him why he got to eat lobster and crab, and we didn't to eat anything, but I was afraid. I remember one time he was eating in front of us, and I got angry and left the room. Under my breath, I called him "wrinkle-neck" and he almost heard me. He stopped me, and asked me what I said. I lied and said "nothing." He said, "Boy, you'ed betta bring yo narra-ass ova hea. Don't make me ask you again, and you betta not lie." I told him, "Wrinkle-neck" and he made me get in the basement and wait for him. I didn't take long for him to come down and beat me.

Sometimes, after a beating, Debbie would come down stairs to check on me. I was about 18 months older than her, but she was always smarter than me. I didn't worry that much about being smart; I wanted to be a good athlete and to be tough. Being a good athlete meant that my dad would be proud of me. Being tough meant that I would suffer fewer beat-downs from my family and neighborhood bullies. It also meant that I could protect my little sister from boys who picked on her. Later in life, I learned that my older sisters needed protection as well, and I never hesitated to administer street-justice to their thug boyfriends once I got old enough to see that three of my four older sisters were in abusive relationships.

I can remember one day when Debbie was playing out in our back yard, and an older boy named Rusty punched her in the stomach, pushed her down, and ran home. Rusty was from a poor white family, and was older than me, about Clarence's age. I saw what he had done, and tried to run him down before he reached his home. He made it to his yard where his vicious dog Sparky, protected him.

Rusty didn't escape justice for long. The next day, Rusty and his siblings were walking down the street in front of our house. Our friend, Donnie lee, we called him Donnalee, one of Mrs. Palmers' boys, who was older than Clarence and younger than Rich, snuck up behind him, covered his mouth and picked him up, and carried him back to the side of our house where Clarence, Debbie and me were waiting. He was kicking his legs, but he couldn't scream to alert his family. We held him while Debbie got in a few licks before we took over and made him pay. We took turns, Clarence launched a vicious attack on him, the kind I had come to know over the years, punching Rusty in the face, giving him two black eyes and a bloody nose, before I took over and landed several blows myself. By the time we were through, Rusty was bruised, battered, and doubled over with pain. He lay on the ground whimpering like a hurt dog. Debbie's licks may not have hurt him much, but he learned there were consequences if put his hands on her again. From that day on, he crossed the street if he saw her playing outside. I knew that my little sister might go to bed hungry every night, but I also knew that if anyone tried to harm her, they were going to pay.

GOING TO CHURCH

I remember going to church. Our neighborhood church, Mesa Hills Bible Church, was an independent affiliated church that glorified God, and honored the testimony of Jesus Christ. It was a mostly white church, with roots in our neighborhood since 1891. Some of my older brothers and sisters went to Payne Chapel African Methodist Episcopal Church that was established in 1872 when Colorado was still a territory. Payne Chapel was the first established place of worship for persons of color in Colorado Springs. It was some distance from our house, so my parents sent the younger kids to Mesa Hills. We worshiped God, and sang the hymns right along with white folks, most of the time from the balcony. We wore our best clothes, and went to church almost every Sunday. My mom usually gave us a few coins to put in the offering plate; sometimes not. When she didn't, we passed the plate down our row, and handed it to the usher at the end.

I liked going to church and learning about God. The stories were almost always fascinating, and we often got to watch a wide variety of them played out on T.V. around Easter and Christmas. We learned about the Old Testament and the Ten Commandments. In the Bible, it seemed like God was powerful, but I was awed when I saw the Ten Commandments on T.V. My dad bought a new color T.V., and when God used fire to carve the Ten Commandment out of stone, it showed just how powerful he really was. I also liked the part when he parted the Red Sea to save the Hebrews that Moses led out of Egypt. My mom told me that her family was from Egypt and crossed the Red Sea with Moses. When I asked her how she knew, she told me that the day her mother died, she had trouble sleeping when a calm came over her and she heard a voice say "fear not, you are a child of God." She said that her experience was so vivid and clear that it frightened her. She told me that when she closed her eyes, she saw a vision of her family leaving Egypt as part of the exodus. I guess we had to come from somewhere in Africa, and Egypt was as good a place as any to be from, so I believed her.

I also learned about the stories in the New Testament, and that all the books of the Bible were inspired words of God. I learned that Jesus was the son of God, and our savior, and that faith in God alone was all that we needed to be saved from our sins. My mom told me that we also had to confess our sins, and ask for forgiveness first. At our house, we made sure that we closed each prayer with "in Jesus' name we pray, Amen."

Another one of the important lessons that I can remember learning at church was that we should use our lives to bear witness to the word of God, and to the truth of the Holy Scriptures in the Bible. I talked to my mom about what some of those lessons meant, and she told me that it meant that I shouldn't cheat or steal and that I should always tell the truth. I think she probably didn't know, but wanted to make sure that I didn't cheat or steal, and that she wanted me to tell the truth.

Easter was always a special day for us. It was one of the few times that I remember getting new clothes. We all piled into the family station wagon, went to J.C. Penny's or Learners, and got new suits or dresses to wear. I always tried to get a different color suit than my brother Clarence, because we were close in size for much of our childhood years and people always got us mixed up with each other. After we got new clothes to wear, the best part of Easter Sunday, even better than the Easter egg hunts, was going to church at Sun Rise Services at the Garden of the Gods. When that sun came up over those red rocks, I could really feel the presence of God. Garden of the Gods sits right at the base of Pikes Peak, and surely, it must have taken the power of God to create such a majestic, spiritual place. The sky was powder blue, the air was cool and crisp, and the orange and red pastel colors of the sunrise were breathtakingly magnificent.

Christmas at our house was special too. My dad usually gave us $5 to buy gifts with, and we headed down to Woolworth's to go shopping. We each had ten gifts to buy, and no one wanted to leave anyone out. Come Christmas Day, we had so many gifts under our tree that you could hardly get into the living room. Our parents usually made us go to bed after we got to see NORAD tracking Santa Clause on the radar. When we woke up, as early as we could Christmas morning, they let us open gifts, and Santa always came while we were asleep. I cried when my older brothers and sisters told me that my mom and dad were really Santa. I remember sitting on Santa's lap, and him giving me a Magic Tunnel. I didn't know for sure if they were right about Santa until I spotted presents in the back of our station wagon on Christmas Eve. Every once in a while, even my older brothers and sisters got it right, there was no Santa.

I am not sure how much difference it made for my older brother and sisters to have gone to a black church and us younger kids to a white church because we all ended up believing in the same God. As near as I could tell, my oldest brother Joe had a good relationship with the Pastor at Payne Chapel, and we really didn't get to know our white Pastor. What I do know is that we had to integrate our neighborhood schools, and we got a chance to worship God with the very same people who we would be going to school with.

Part II

Special Education and Athletic Competition

CHAPTER 2

SPECIAL EDUCATION

For years, school districts across the country have struggled to educate students with learning disabilities. In 1966, School District 11 in Colorado Springs was no different. I found out that I was a slow learner, the hard way, in front of my classmates in school. Helen Hunt was the first school I remember attending. We didn't go there long before we transferred to Bristol Meyers Elementary School. Bristol was our neighborhood school and it had a higher concentration of Black and Latino students in attendance than other area schools.

We were new to the area and often fought with other children at Bristol. We fought so much, that the school district told our parents that we could attend Zebulon Pike Elementary School, a predominantly white school, about a mile from our house. There were two disadvantages that we faced attending Pike, a school bus took us to Bristol, and we had to walk to Pike. Second, our family, along with four or five other black families, helped integrate predominantly white elementary, junior high, and high schools on the western part of the city.

At our new school, many of my teachers seemed nice, the books were newer, and we had to make new friends. One of our biggest problems was walking to school through predominately-white neighborhoods, and having some white people treat us badly because we looked different. We were black, our clothes were often oversized hand-me-downs or ragged, and the shoes we wore were so ragged that we had to use cutout cardboard for soles.

David Caruth, back row, 2nd from right. Integrating Zebulon
Pike Elementary School, Colorado Springs, Colorado, 1968.

After we left home for school, we were always hungry, even after eating
a miniature box of cereal for breakfast or sometimes a half grapefruit. We
often ate what little lunch our mom prepared for us on the way to school.
We stopped along the way and picked fruit off our neighbor's fruit trees,
ate rhubarb, and raided trashcans for discarded food. When wild fruit was
not available, sometimes we stopped by the local Quick Mart and helped
ourselves to food, without paying. At school, sometimes I visited my
classmates' lunch pails that were kept in the hallway.

Our dad was a proud man, to proud to accept welfare. Sometimes we
left for school without lunch because there was nothing to make lunch with
at our house. My dad brought our lunches to school in a full size grocery
bag to disguise the fact that all he really delivered was a square of four
saltine crackers, with butter on them, for each of us. When the principal
called us to the office to get our lunches, we opened the bag, looked inside,
and cried. We were starving.

Many times, we fought our way through their neighborhoods, and
often had to run when people sicked their dogs on us. My speed came in
handy as we ran to escape being bitten by dogs. I took to carrying a stick

with me to and from school so that I could defend myself from bigger kids, and fight off the dogs.

In school, I learned that I could barely read and write and that I had to attend Special Education classes for slow learners. I was embarrassed, ashamed, and endured humiliating taunts from my classmates. My new friends and nemeses alike, smirked as I was excused from the classroom during reading and writing, to spend time with the Special Ed teacher. Had I gone to Bristol, my academic performance may have been considered normal, and I would have joined the ranks of millions of other poor, disadvantaged children in our society that get passed along from grade to grade without being properly educated. Walking to the white school, through the white neighborhood, and attending special education classes turned out be a blessing.

In my Special Ed class, I struggled to read aloud, and none of the other slow learners made fun of me. My Special Ed teacher encouraged me to sound out words, and taught me how to understand punctuation marks. He also tried to teach me how to spell, which I never quite learned. The lessons were hard, but he was patient. He also taught me how to write. Reading and writing were my toughest subjects to learn. I struggled with those subjects throughout my life, at each stage of my education, and even today. Learning math, on the other hand, now that was a different story.

My teachers soon learned that I had exceptional math skills. For whatever reason, it didn't impress them that I calculated answers to math problems, in my head, faster than their favorite students arrived at the correct answers with pencil and paper. When my teacher asked a math question, my hand shot up immediately. She often overlooked me, giving her favorite students time to calculate their answers.

After my teacher didn't call on me to answer questions, day after day after day, and my classmates received praise for getting the right answer, my competitive juices boiled over, and I took matters into my own hands. Determined to get noticed, and receive praise for solving math problems correctly, I raised my had and blurted out the correct answer so many times that my teacher became annoyed, and punished me, instead of giving me the praise that I so desperately needed to improve my self-esteem, and build a positive self-image.

On test after test, I finished first and handed in my test with most, if not all, of the questions answered correctly. Rather than accept my answers, my teachers accused me of having cheated because I answered my questions correctly, without having showed the process I used to arrive at my answers. She knew that I had a calculator in my head because I arrived at the correct answer in class before my classmates could copy down the problem. When I protested against being falsely accused of cheating, she sent me down to the principal's office for punishment. All of my friends knew that my being sent to the principals' office meant a phone call home and a beating when I got there. I took the long way home.

By the time I arrived home, it was beginning to get dark. My school clothes were covered with dirt and mud as I went creek-walking on the way home. The cardboard in my shoes gave way to the water and my feet were exposed through holes in my sox, which were blackened by dirt. I was filthy, hungry, and ready for my beating. I tried to slip in through the back door and go down stairs to my bedroom without being heard. No such luck. The moment I cracked opened the back door, the family alarm system went off, "David's home." I cursed to myself, and went down stairs to my room. My mom worked nights, and my dad didn't disappoint.

The strange thing about my dad was the he never had time to talk to me, but he liked to talk to me as he beat me with his thin, black leather belt. He was much bigger than me, and when he grabbed my arm, it was as if someone tightened a vice around it. Right before he beat me, my dad would say things like "boy, this is gonna hurt me more than it's gonna hurt you" or he would say "boy, you know I'm gonna have to skin you alive" and he practically did too. The black and blue whelps across my back and legs would be noticeable for weeks at a time, and were clearly visible during gym class where I had to wear shorts. He beat me so bad that my legs bled.

While still whimpering on the floor, as my dad turned to leave the room, I managed to tell him that if the beating I took hurt him more than it hurt me, he must be crazy. He wasn't impressed, and returned and beat me some more. Those extra licks hurt more because he stood over me and swung his belt as hard as he could and hit any part of my body that was exposed. He wasted no motion, hitting me first with a forehand motion and then by his backhand, several time without stopping. When he was done, he asked me if I had anything else to say. Satisfied that I didn't, he turned to walk out of my room again. I should have been smarter and kept my mouth shut, but I wasn't smart, I was in Special Ed, so I said "yes." When he turned around, I said, "I hate you. When I get bigger than you, I'm gonna beat you!" He must have believed me, because he returned and beat me some more. I tried to cover my face and head to keep from getting hit there. I ended up with whelps on my body from the neck down.

After getting beat, there was no dinner for me that night. Someone else had eaten my share of the food. I sat on the basement stairs, hungry and in pain. My mom knew I was there, and snuck me a piece of fried chicken that she managed to save. I gobbled it up, and gave the bone to my trusty dog Sampson through my bedroom window. Sampson was always hungry, and happy to see me, he was my friend. On many a night after a beating, I hugged my silver colored German Shepherd, and went to bed hungry. On that particular night, I was glad that I got to eat, even though it meant that my mom had given me her dinner, and went to bed hungry herself.

After learning about my being accused of cheating at school, my mom taught me another one of her lessons. She taught me that what goes on in the dark would one day come to the light. I really didn't know what she meant at the time, but she always had a way of teaching me through parables or passages from the Bible. I tried to understand, but this time I didn't.

Later on that year, my teacher gave the class an I.Q. test. I took mine, and my mom came to school to learn my results. My teacher sat with my mom and me, and told us that my reading and writing skills were well below average, and that I still needed to attend Special Ed; however, she also had to report that I was a genius in math. She made no apology to me, but I could tell that it pained her to have to tell my mom my math scores, in front of me, after she had publicly humiliated me in class. I thought my moms' parable meant that someone would expose my dad for beating me, but what happened was that I got praise for my math skills after being labeled a cheater. I wasn't a cheater, my mom was proud of me, and I was proud of myself as well. To me, that's all that mattered.

For the remainder of the year, and many years thereafter, I went to Special Ed and did my best to learn how to read, write and spell. It would be years before I learned to read and write well enough to learn alongside my classmates. All the while, I was embarrassed and ashamed, because I desperately wanted to be smart like my brothers and sisters and my classmates. My one saving grace was math. I continued to irritate my teachers who, for whatever reason, didn't call on me to answer math problems. By now, they knew that I was a slow learner, but they also knew that God had given me a special gift, a calculator in my brain.

Standing Up to the School Bully

By the time I was seven years old, my older brother Clarence started calling me Mean Gene. Gene was a comic strip character, an elephant that always got mad, and stomped on the lion in the strip. The name fit. I was mean. I don't think I was born mean, deformed and slow maybe, but not mean. I learned to become mean, because I had to defend myself on a daily basis, and I did.

I had gotten used to running through the white neighborhoods, going to and from school, but my speed failed me as a defense at Pike. The school bully in my class didn't appreciate opening his lunch pail only to find that his sandwich was missing, along with his special treat. Bill learned that I raided his lunch pail, and he challenged me to meet him after school at the sand lot, to settle things. I didn't know whose lunch pail it was that I raided, but as it turned out, Bill was much larger than me, and the buzz around school was that he was going to pound me. I thought he might pound me too; however, by then I had already taken many poundings from my older brothers and sisters. My dad also made it clear to us that we had better not come home without fighting if someone called us out; because if we did, he was going to beat us. I went into my secret place at school, next to the janitors' closet, and prayed to God for courage and strength.

After school, Bill and I met at the sandlot, and the other second grade boys quickly encircled us. There was no way for me to hit Bill and run. Bill was hungry, and angry that I had eaten his lunch, and he attacked me. As skinny as I was, I couldn't have withstood the force of his blow. I used my quickness, to side-step his lunge and escape his grasp. Using Bills force against him; I balled-up my fist, and swung with all of my might. As he went by, I landed a powerful blow that hit Bill in his stomach. He fell to the ground in pain. Unable to breath, he gasped for air. My punch knocked the air out of him. I stood over Bill; fists balled up, and challenged him to get up. Like David and Goliath, I took down the giant with a single blow. God had answered my prayer.

My friends cheered, and Bill's friends looked on, shocked and dismayed. After the fight, Bill stopped crying and got to his feet. Several of his friends wanted to attack me too. One glance from Bill changed their minds. He made it clear to all of us, that if I could beat him, I could beat them. From that day on, I was the school bully and I made it known, that if any of them wanted a piece of me, they had to fight Bill first. No one wanted to fight Bill, and I beat him fair and square.

After the big fight, Herral, his little brother Terry, and I walked home from school in triumph. Debbie usually walked home behind us with her friends. Herral and Terry knew I was tough, but not that tough. They patted me on the back, vied to be my best friend, and retold the story of the punch that put Bill down, complete with simulations that included rolling around on the ground holding their bellies. Herral had a knack for retelling stories, complete with sound effects and visuals, including how big my eyes got when Bill attacked me. The funny thing was that they didn't seem to care how dirty they got. Herral and Terry rolled around on the ground, holding their bellies, with their school clothes on, and boy did they look funny.

The next day at school, the buzz was going around that I beat-up Bill. Students and teachers alike were all stunned. When I got called into the principal's office to offer my account of the fight, I told him that Bill and I were friends. He called Bill into his office too, and Bill agreed with me. I don't know if we had character, or if we were lying to protect ourselves, but it worked and we did become friends after that. What I knew for sure, was that if I got kicked out of school for fighting, I was getting whipped when I got home.

On the weekends, everyone in our house had to get-up and clean-up. My sisters had to clean their rooms and the inside of the house and my brothers and I had to clean up the basement before my dad ordered us outside to pick up everything that didn't grow. Many times, my dog Sampson would have escaped his leash, knocked over a trashcan or two, and left the evidence spewed across our back yard. After we finished picking up the yard, my mom made sure that we pulled the weeds from her garden before we got permission to disappear into the neighborhood.

Always hungry and looking for something to do, I noticed that a little old lady, who lived down the alley from our house, had a garden similar to my mom's. Her garden was overgrown with weeds, and I asked her if she wanted me to pull them out of her garden. She was pleased that I had asked, and said yes. Pulling weeds for the old lady became my first paid job. My mom taught me how to weed a garden, and I used my skills on the old lady's garden as well. The old lady was as pleased as my mom, and she paid me thirty-five cents for my efforts. Back in 1967, candy cost a penny and you could buy a bottle of pop for a nickel. I walked down past the nursery that was a block away from our house, on to the 7-11 store, and bought penny candy, a Big Hunk, and a bottle of strawberry soda too. Life was good, at least for a moment.

Later that day, when I saw my mom and told her about my new job, she was so proud of me. She told me that I should always treat old people good, and that they would be good to me. I offered her a piece of candy and she accepted. I think I got my sweet tooth from her, because she had false teeth and had to put them in to eat. She told me that if I didn't brush my teeth, my teeth would fall out just like hers. I hurried up stairs and brushed my teeth.

GONE FISHING

On the weekends, I did my chores at home and worked for the old lady down the alley to earn money. I also learned that my dad had been taking my older brothers fishing at Prospect Lake. When I asked him about it, he took me too, and taught me how to fish. When we got to the lake, he took an old Zebco 404 out of this tackle box, repaired it, and showed me how to attach it to an old fishing pole that had several eyes missing. He gave me a lesson or two on how to cast my line, and then sent me packing to the other side of the lake because I crossed his line while casting my line into the water. It wouldn't have been so bad if the other side of the lake was not a mile away. I also had to leave the night crawlers that I caught for him as bait the night before. My dad and brothers didn't catch any fish that day. When I got to the other side of the lake, white people were there boating, so I watched them having fun and skipped a few flat stones across the water. On my dad's side of the lake, not throwing stones in the water was the first rule of fishing. While I was on the other side of the lake, he sent my brothers to the 7-11 for snacks and didn't bother to save any for me.

I didn't catch any fish that day either, but I learned a valuable skill that I could enjoy for a lifetime, and one that I passed along to my own kids later on in life. Over the years, my dad sent me packing to the other side of the lake many times. The good news was that he continued to take me fishing, and I brought my own worms to fish with.

The next morning, I got up early and me and my dog Sampson walked to the frog pond to do a little fishing. I still had worms left over from the previous day. The frog pond was a little pond that had a little island in the center of it, about mile from our house. Until I learned how to fish,

I went to the pond to catch frogs. My dad was right about how to fish. I caught 57, 2-inch long, Blue Gills. They were so small, that after we fried them, we ate the whole fish without having to remove the bones. My dad ate some too and he had a big smile on his face. I couldn't tell if he was proud of me for catching so many fish, or if the size of the fish I caught amused him. Any way you looked at it, lesson learned and we had a fish fry that night.

My Pet Snake

That same year, my friends, Herral, Terry and I were becoming closer friends. They were from Mobile and Herral told me all sorts of stories about being from the country. They dressed in overalls and got mad when I called them farmers. Herral gave me a history lesson about how important farmers were to our way of life. I couldn't disagree with him, so we took off, the three of us and my dog Sampson, exploring the foothills behind our homes.

We walked for miles, exploring the creeks, hills, and valleys in our neighborhood. We looked under rocks, pieces of wood, and discarded debris that other people had dumped in the foothills. We found strange looking bugs and other animals. All of us loved animals. I turned over a piece of plywood and out crawled a baby snake. I caught it and took it home in my pocket. I showed it to my older brothers Rich and Clarence and to Herral and Terry's older brother, Donnalee. We agreed that it was a baby bull snake. It was light brown, about five inches long, and wasn't very friendly. No matter, I carried that snake around in my pocket. It was my friend. I planned to take the snake with me to school the next day, for show and tell. Almost all of my white friends brought all sorts of pets to school for show and tell, and I wanted to show off my new snake.

That evening, my mom saw how dirty I was and insisted that I take a bath before going to bed. I went up stairs to take my bath and dropped my dirty clothes down the chute, snake in pocket, and all. Sometimes, if I timed it right, I could drop my dirty laundry on my sisters' heads as they sorted the dirty laundry. No luck this time, but there would be other times, lots of them, when my dirty clothes would hit the target.

The next morning, I got the same dirty pants out of the dirty clothes to wear to school that day. I thought my snake was still in the pocket for show and tell. I was surprised when I got to school that day. My mom called the principal and told him to send her boys home because there was a snake loose in the house. My brother Clarence was out of school first and running for home. I know, because when I got the message, I took off, like a greyhound, running down the street headed for home. After about two blocks of running, I passed him. He was moving out, too, but he had asthma so he had to stop and walk every now and then. By the fifth block, Clarence later told me, that I disappeared out of his sight.

When I got home, I came in through the back door to find my mom frightened out of her mind. When she was mad, she didn't call us by our names, or even boy, it was "Niggaaaa." I didn't wait to hear the rest, because I knew I was in trouble. I also knew where the snake must have been, in the laundry, and I could hear her mumbling something about the laundry anyway on my way downstairs to the laundry room. Within a matter of minute, and before Clarence made it home, I found the snake and returned it to its home, in my pocket. I tried to show it to my mom, but she didn't want to see it. She just wanted it out of her house. When I was leaving through the back door, I could hear her saying, "Niggaaaa, you betta get that….." I tried not to hear the rest.

When I went outside, I saw Clarence rounding the corner to our street. When he finally reached our yard, I told him that my pet snake had escaped my pocket, but that I caught it. He made me show it to him before he believed me. I wasn't surprised that he wanted to see the snake because my mom had taught us to trust, but verify. Mom always told me that she taught him the same lessons that she taught me. He went inside to comfort our mom. When he was satisfied, that our mom was all right, he came outside and we walked back to school. He wasn't happy that our mom was frightened by my snake or that he got called out of school, but the story he told about how fast I was running when I passed him, made us both laugh.

THE BULLET WOUND

One weekend, me and Herral went down the alley to pull weeds for my old lady. She was happy to see me and agreed to give us a dollar to pull the weeds out of her garden in the backyard, and out of her flowers in the front. We agreed. After we pulled the weeds, Herral got mad and refused to accept his share of the money, twenty-five cents, because he thought he should get half. I disagreed. Pulling weeds for the old lady was my job, and his share was a quarter for helping. I told him that I could have pulled all the weeds myself, and kept all the money. He went home mad and refused to accept his share of the money.

Later that day, Rich, Donnalee, Clarence, Terry and I went to 7-11 to spend the money. Herral stayed home. On the way, we decided to throw rocks at bullets that I took from my dad's room. My dad owned a 22-caliber rifle, and kept a box of shells in his drawer. I helped myself to a few of them. We put the bullets on the railroad tracks and threw rocks at them. I was a pretty good rock thrower, and hit my bullet. It fired. We were all excited by the sound of it going off. At the same time the sound of the shot rang out, I felt something hot hit my calf. I put my hand down to rub it and my hand came back bloody. We were all terrified. I managed to shoot myself in the leg. My brother Rich looked on as Donnalee ripped the shirt right off his back, tore it into strips, and bandaged my leg as best he could. The blood kept flowing.

Rich and Donnalee tried to carry me home, but they were too weak, or the dead weight of my skeleton body was too heavy. Right when they put me down and told me that I had to walk, our dad drove by and yelled out of his car window "git home." When we got home, my dad whipped all of us. My mom was furious that he took time to whip me, while my leg bled. She loaded me into the car and took me the base hospital at Fort Carson. On the way to the hospital, I got lightheaded and almost went to sleep. Every time my eyelids got close to staying closed, I kept hearing my mom say, "Don't go to sleep baby, you have to stay awake." I didn't know why she wanted me to stay awake, but I did. My mom worked as a nurse's aide and told me later that she thought that I lost so much blood, that if I went to sleep, I might have slipped into a coma or maybe even died. They admitted me into the emergency room to stop the bleeding and to remove the slug.

After the surgery, I learned that the bullet had severed a large vein in my calf and lodged itself in between the tibia and fibulas bones in my leg. A fraction of an inch to the left or the right, the doctor told me, the slug would have broken a bone in my leg. After removing the slug and seeing the whelps on my legs, the doctor told my mom that if she wasn't my custodial parent, they would have locked her up in the stockade. Instead, they let her take me home.

When I got home, I was tired and went to bed. I couldn't sleep that night because I could hear screaming and yelling and things breaking up stairs. Every now and then, I could hear some of the cuss words that my mom was using, and I thought I heard her say that my dad was lucky that she didn't kill him. If you knew my mom, you also knew that she might have done it if the doctors didn't fix my bullet wound. When I thought about it, if the bullet had broken my leg, I wouldn't have been able to walk and may have died out there on the street that day. My dad didn't stop to see how badly I was injured when he yelled at us to get home. This was the second time that I escaped death.

CHAPTER 3

1968 THE TURBULENT YEAR OF CHANGE

All sorts of things happened in 1968. My dad retired from the Army and was angry that someone assassinated Bobby Kennedy. I think he was upset because someone killed his brother, President John F. Kennedy, a few years earlier. He was happy that Apollo 8, and astronaut Jim Lovell, went to the moon. He was mad that people protested at the Democratic convention in Chicago. He got even angrier when Americans elected Richard Millhouse Nixon, as President of the United States. I didn't really know what all of those events meant, but they were on T.V. and I got to watch them with my dad. While all those events were taking place, what troubled me the most was that someone assassinated Martin Luther King, Jr. I couldn't figure out why anyone would want to kill him. He went to jail a whole bunch of times without putting up a fight.

That same year, the relationships in our family changed as well. My older brother Rich, who used to let me hang around him, helped his friends torture me. One day, when I was playing football in our back yard with my friends, he helped hold me down while his friend Keith, stood over me, and let spit ooze down from his mouth, and get close to my face before sucking it back up. Keith was a big white boy, and there was no way for me hit him and run. He was big, strong and fast. I didn't really know how I could get Rich back, so I vowed to take my revenge on Keith.

Since I couldn't hit Keith and run, I planned to stick a knife in his back with a blade I found while creek-walking. The knife was beautiful. It was round, and looked like a pencil painted with Japanese designs and writing. Hidden inside, there was a six-inch long, razor-sharp blade that I could remove and insert back into the handle, making a dangerous knife.

One day, Keith was standing by a tree in our backyard, and not paying any attention to me. I took the painted stick out of my pocket, affixed the knife, and plunged the blade towards his back. Rich caught my wrist just before it reached Keith's back. Keith saw what I tried to do to him, and left me alone after that. Rich started respecting me a little more after that too. He knew I was fearless, but now he was sure that I would use a deadly weapon to hurt someone.

My relationship with my oldest brother Joe also changed. Joe wasn't around much, but when he came around, he enforced his own brand of justice. Joe didn't beat me down to many times, but I remember one day when me and my friends were playing basketball in the backyard. He interrupted our game because he and his friends wanted to play. I refused to give up the court, and told him to wait until we were done. The rules of the court were that he could call the next game, and his team could play the winner. Rather than wait, he and his friends held me down and punched me in the thigh until I cried. I took several hard punches before I gave in. Joe wasn't that big, but his friends, David, Steve, Rodney, and John were huge. My friends and I surrendered the court. I thought about throwing rocks at them, and didn't. I had to find another way to get him back.

The next day, Joe agreed to pay me if I helped him deliver papers on his paper route. He always gave me the hills on his route because he didn't want to peddle his bike up the hills. When I got home after delivering the papers, he didn't even pay me. He told me that our mom took his money. I asked my mom if she took his money and she said no. She told me not to get mad, but to get even.

The next time Joe asked me to deliver his papers up the hills, I agreed. Only this time, Joe got a call to deliver the papers on the hills later on in the day. When he went to deliver the papers he found that I had thrown the papers that I was supposed to deliver in a kennel where a vicious dog lived. I felt justified because he didn't pay me last time, kicked me off the basketball court, and helped his friends punch me in the thigh. The next day, he refused to let me eat some Kentucky Fried Chicken that he brought home from work, and I had to go to bed hungry that night.

My two oldest sisters, Pam and Genie, didn't beat me much, they did other things like pinched my skin to get me to move off the coach so they could sit down. They also made fun of me. I had a habit of rubbing my lips, and they went out of their way to make me feel bad because of it. They were too old for me to fight, but I told on them a lot. Sometimes, they got in trouble, sometimes not. When they didn't, I made runs in their stockings, and listened for them to blame each other. Getting even was getting even.

FIGHTING IT OUT WITH MY FRIENDS

It had been two years since I beat up Bill, and both Herral and Terry had gotten taller and stronger. In our neighborhood, your rep only lasted so long, so we fought to determine who would be the leader of our group. I fought Terry first. Terry always tried to intimidate other boys by his size and talking tough. If that didn't work, he'd try to pushing and shoving boys to get them to back down, without fighting. As soon as he opened his mouth, I attacked him with lightning fast speed, and delivered a hard right to his nose, and a left to his jaw, before I took him down to the ground. I put a chokehold on him, and choked him until he gave. He was stunned. I left him lying in the dirt, crying, wondering what happened.

Beating Herral was another matter. Herral was tall, taller than Terry, had large hands, and was nearly as strong as me. He saw what I just done to his little brother, and wasted no time attacking me. When he swung on me with his long arms and huge fists, it was as if he tied a rock on a rope, swung it around his head for speed, and then hit me with it. After absorbing a rock-fist to the temple area of my head, I tackled Herral, wrestled him to the ground, delivered two hard blows to temple area of his head, and bent his arm behind his back to make him give. I pushed the arm back until tears came streaming down his face. He cried silent tears without making a sound.

Herral was tough, and wouldn't agree to stop fighting. When I let him up, he hit me with another one of those rock-fists. I delivered several blows of my own to his gut and nose. I even drew first blood, but he just wouldn't quit. He delivered several more blows to my head, before I wrestled him to the ground again. He finally gave when I put the headlock on him and choked him. I was so angry because his punches hurt a lot. I would have choked him to death if his older brother hadn't of pulled me off him. I beat both of them, but I didn't want to tangle with Herral again. I am sure that he didn't want to tangle with me again either. In fact, we never fought again. We were friends again, best friends, and I was the leader. Years later, we would grow apart, but for now, I was in charge.

Until then, my friends and I made decisions about where to go and what to do by talking. Most of the time, the group followed my lead because I was unafraid and adventurous. That year, even my new friend, Eddie, questioned my authority to decide where we went and what we did when we got there. Eddie's bravado was curious because he was two years younger than me, he was shorter too, and kind of chubby. He caught me on the wrong day. I was already angry, angry at the world for treating me bad. I was angry because Malcolm X and Dr. King got killed. I was angry because my relationships with my older brothers worsened; however, most of all, I was angry that my new friend, who was two years younger than me, had the nerve to challenge my authority to lead our group. Herral and Terry looked at Eddie like he was crazy, and Herral even asked him if he was crazy. Eddie was brave because he had two older brothers, and thought he was tough.

Eddie squared up on me and I greeted him with a lightning quick, vicious attack. I struck him in the mouth with a hard left and in the jaw with a hard right. I grabbed him by the throat, and I hit him twice in the gut, before I grabbed him by the head, and flipped him to ground using a judo move that I learned from my brother Joe. I put him in the headlock and delivered three more hard lefts to his nose. I squeezed his head for another minute or two before letting him up. In the end, my attack left him bloodied and crying on the ground.

The pent-up anger inside me exploded, and my other friends looked on and witnessed the devastating attack that I had just unleashed a split second ago. My adrenaline got the better of me, and I got up and asked my other friends, "Does anyone else want a piece of me?" There were no takers. I was glad that there were no takers because they would have met the same fate, and I may have lost some friends for good. I changed that day, from following my older brothers around, to becoming the leader of my own group of friends.

At school, I talked so much trash, and pushed weaker boys around so much, that they started telling their big brothers on me. One day, an eighth grader came down to the elementary school and waited for me after school. He was planning to teach me a lesson, and make sure that I left his little brother alone. I saw his little brother point me out to him, and he called out to me. I turned on the jets. He chased me home that day, at least part of the way, because we both ran into my older brother Clarence who had gotten kicked out of school, and was walking home. Clarence had gotten kicked out of school for beating up a kid who was making fun of one of our other friends, Donny, who had a mental disability. He was in a bad mood already because he knew that he was going to get whipped when he got home for getting kicked out of school. When Clarence saw me being chased, he wasn't having any of it. He was short, but he was also a good wrestler and strong for his size. He took the boy down in flash and put a hurting on him. By the time he let the boy up; Clarence put two black eyes and a bloody nose on him.

THE GOOD AND THE BAD IN MY COMMUNITY

I was eight years old when Herral and I went down to my old lady's house in search of work. She wasn't home, so we decided to play on mounds of dirt at the Nursery across the street from her house. The owner was a nice old man who had a neck problem. He couldn't move his neck like normal people, and had to turn his body, to look in different directions. He saw Herral and me playing at his nursery and ordered us off his property. We should have left, but I had a different idea. I told Herral that we could throw grenades, AKA dirt clods, at the owner. We ducked behind a mound of dirt, pretended to pull the pins out of our grenades, and launched them over the hill at the old man, without looking. After we threw them, looked up to see how close we came to hitting him. We never did hit him, but some of our grenades exploded close to him. He retreated into the nursery, and we ran down the alley back home.

That night, he paid a visit to my house, and he was angry. He told my mom what I had done, before going next door to tell Herral's mom what he had done. I saw him leaving and knew that I was going to get beat that evening when my dad got home. I stayed outside, hiding in my dog Sampson's doghouse, until late into the night. I ignored my mom's calls for me to come in for hours.

When I finally came in, I snuck down the stairs, only to find my dad waiting for me in my room. He was fuming and his belt was already off. I started to cry, but he told me, "Boy, tears aint gonna protect you from this ass-whoppin." He beat me good that night. All the while, he was beating me he assured me that he wasn't going to stop until his arm fell off. Well, it didn't fall off. After getting beat for about fifteen or twenty minute, I stopped trying to escape and fell to the ground. He finally got tired of holding me up with one arm and beating me with the other, and stopped. I earned that beating, and I got it too. I also got to go to bed hungry, again.

The next day, Herral and I compared notes. He said he heard me screaming for what seemed like hours. I agreed with him, and showed him the black and blue whelps on my back and legs to prove it. He told me that his mom pulled his ear and said that he couldn't play with me anymore. He told me that she said I was a bad influence on him. She may have been right, but we laughed at the idea of not playing together. It was also funny that she pulled his ear because he had big ears, and they would have been easy to grab and pull. I pointed that out to him, and said that the ear on the left side of his head was larger than the one on the right side. We laughed and went to Monument Valley Park.

WILD PETS

Monument Valley Park was a nice park where people went to picnic, play tennis, jog, walk, swim, play basketball and feed the ducks that gathered around a manmade lake that had a little island in the middle of it. It also had a little baseball diamond and a creek that ran past it. At the Park, white people were feeding the ducks and they waddled right up to us. We couldn't believe how friendly the ducks were and I got a bright idea. I told Herral that we could grab a couple of ducks, take them home, and tell our parents that they followed us home. He agreed, and we did it. We each snatched a duck and took off running. I was faster than Herral, but we both got away anyway.

When we got home, we asked our moms if we could keep them. My mom asked where the ducks came from and I told her our story, that we were feeding the ducks and that they followed us home. I don't know what Herral's mom said to him, but my mom didn't buy it and made me tell her the truth. I told her the truth and she let me keep the duck. Herral's mom let him keep his duck as well. I named my duck, Duck and Herral named his duck, Duck-duck.

The next weekend, my friends Herral, Terry, Eddie and I went looking to capture pigeons from underneath bridges. The bridges were high, and it was dangerous, but we scaled our way to the top from underneath. We caught some and put them in a pigeon coop that Herral and Terry's brother Butch built for his pigeons. In addition to catching a few pigeons, I also caught a bat and brought it home. We all agreed that it needed to be stored in a dark place so I put it in my mom's washing machine and closed the lid. I had planned to take it out by nightfall, but ended up going to bed before I did. In the morning, I went to school as usual. On the way to school, my friends and I talked about our pets, picked some fruit off our neighbors' trees for our lunch, and stopped by the Quick Mart to pick up a few pieces of candy. Sometimes, I helped myself to candy when the store clerk wasn't looking, but this time, I had a dollar to spend because I worked for my old lady down the alley.

By the time I arrived at school, my mom had called and told the principal to send her boys home. Before the principal could get out why, I already knew, and set out for home at top speed. I made it home in five or six minutes. It took about the same amount of time drive that distance. I busted in through the back door, went down stairs, and got the jelly jar that I had planned to put the bat in the night before. When I opened the washing machine door, the bat spread its wings and was larger than I remembered. I closed the lid. I needed a plan. I turned the machine on cold water for a few seconds and then opened the lid. The bat had returned to its normal size, I grabbed it, put it in the jar, and took it to school. The principal refused to let me display it in show and tell and made me let it go. I did and it hung upside down outside the school building that day, and disappeared into the night.

A few weeks later, Herral, Terry, Eddie and I went back to the foothills to see if we could catch more snakes. Most of the time, we caught garden snakes, but sometimes, we caught bull snakes. We liked bull snakes better because they got bigger than garden snakes. I spotted a snake that was moving faster than most of the snakes that we usually caught, as it went under a piece of wood. I knew that I would have to react quickly to catch this snake, and I asked Herral to lift the wood. When he lifted it, I snatched the snake by the head, just like I'd done with other snakes. It was a good-sized snake, and it was more powerful than the other snakes that I caught. I carried the snake home by its head and put it in our front yard to play with it when it curled up, raised its tail at one end and its head at the other. When it raised its tail and began to shake it, we noticed that it had a couple of rattles on it. I ran inside and got my dad. He killed it with a baseball bat. I think that was the third time that I escaped death.

By the end of the school year, I competed in five track and field activities: the 50-yard dash, the 100-yard dash, the long jump, the high jump, and the standing broad jump. I placed first in all five events and went home the proud owner of five blue ribbons. Both my mom and dad were proud of me, and I received a pat on the head as praise. I earned the right to sit with my dad and watch Gayle Sayers, the famed running back for the Chicago Bears, make unimaginable moves on the football field. I dreamed I could be like him. How hard could it be to become a football player anyway? My mother had already taught me that I could be anything in the world that I wanted to be, all I had to do was work harder than anyone else, and not give up. If sports were what my dad enjoyed watching the most, I would give him sports.

CHAPTER 4

BECOMING THE BEST ATHLETE AT MY SCHOOL

I was interested in sports because that was one of the few ways that I could vie for some of my dad's affection. Beside his habitual pastime activity of gambling-away his money at the dog track, his favorite leisure time activity was watching sports on T.V. He rooted for the Chicago Bears and the Boston Celtics. He also watched track and field and boxing. He hated Howard Cosell, and disagreed with him during most boxing matches. My dad was a Golden Glove boxing champion, so he knew a little bit about that profession.

I liked watching boxing on T.V. My favorite boxer was Muhammad Ali. My dad hated Ali. He called him the Louisville Lip, because he thought he talked too much. He told me that the Clay's and the Caruth's were blood relatives, with both of our families coming from Kentucky. I didn't know whether to believe him or not, but I loved watching Ali fight. I loved his poetry outside the ring, and his boxing inside the ring. I was proud of him and it didn't bother me that most of my white friends hated him. Ali was great, and as he referred to himself, he was the greatest.

My white friends didn't have many white boxing heroes to root for, so they rooted for any boxer who fought Ali. When we played boxing outside in our backyard, I enjoyed pretending to be Ali, and allowing my friends to be any other boxer. Like Ali, I beat all my friends into submission, except for Herral, and then stood over them and talked trash. Herral beat me with the gloves on. I couldn't overcome his height and reach advantage. After he beat me, I was angry and challenged him to fight me without the gloves, he said no.

On track and field day at school, I was winning every event as usual, when the unthinkable happened; Herral out-jumped me in the standing broad jump. I had beaten him three straight years in every event. He was so proud to have finally won a blue ribbon, and silenced the cousin of the Louisville Lip. I walked home alone that day. On the way, I threw my red, second place ribbon in the standing broad jump, in a neighborhood trashcan. I cried my eyes out. I had to be the best athlete in my grade, in every event, and on that particular day, I wasn't. I vowed to never let Herral beat me in athletic competition again. He never did.

That summer, following my loss to my best friend, I trained as though I was training for the Olympics. I stretched, did push-ups and sit-ups, ran, and lifted weights. I practiced every sport I could, and in the end, I improved both my strength and speed. I grew in size and was as big as my older brother Clarence was. I could now out run him with ease and I was beginning to match his strength. My confidence was on the rise and Clarence knew it. I was on my way to becoming a leader, and the best athlete at my school.

Tennis and the Arthur Ashe Affect

Later that summer, Arthur Ashe, the famous African American tennis star, won the U.S. Open Championship. That was an important achievement because his victory exposed my generation to tennis. Until his victory, I thought tennis was a sport for only white athletes. Ashe's victory changed my perception of reality.

One day, we were riding bikes that we made ourselves from discarded parts that people dumped in the foothills behind our house, when Clarence fell off his bike, and nearly got hit by a car driven by the Colorado College Tennis Coach. The coach stopped his car to see if Clarence was hurt. When Clarence said no, he asked Clarence if he was interested in playing tennis that summer. Clarence said yes, but that he had to ask our mom, so the coach gave my brother his phone number.

When we got home, Clarence asked our mom if we could play tennis. She said yes, and called the coach. He was pleased that we were interested in playing tennis, and bought all of us tennis rackets, tennis balls, T-shirts and taught us a few lessons before he resigned his position at Colorado College. Later that summer, the National Junior Tennis League hired a new coach, a strikingly attractive young African American woman, to coach us at Monument Valley Park.

Our new coach was an excellent coach. We played in, and won several matches. My brother Rich was a natural athlete. He and his doubles partner, Donnalee won the doubles championship, and he still has the trophy to prove it. However, my brother Clarence excelled at singles. This was his sport and he could beat most of us. He couldn't out run any of us, beat any of us in basketball, or football, but he sure could beat most of us in tennis. I think he excelled because he was infatuated with the coach. Whatever the reason, he beat me and my friends into submission, and received the most kudos and attention from our coach. There was nothing any of us could do about it. He was the only one of us to go on and play varsity tennis in high school. He took state.

GALE SAYERS AND DICK BUTKUS
ALL ROLLED-UP INTO ONE

That same year, I started playing organized football. My goal was to become the best running back in the American Youth League. At every practice, in every drill, my goal was to come in first. Sometimes I didn't, but I willingly endured the pain of minor injuries, migraine headaches and fatigue trying to be the very best. I gave 110% effort to be the best at my position. If my coaches didn't recognize that I was the best athlete on the team at the beginning of the season, my maximum effort at practice, and play on the field during games, forced them to acknowledge it by season's end.

I was a fierce competitor, and playing football allowed me to take my aggression out on other inspiring athletes, in a controlled environment. My coaches praised me for my speed, and willingness to hit my opponents with reckless abandon; in practice and in games. I became the intimidator. I brought maximum pain on every play. Sometimes, my coaches asked me to ease up on my teammates in practice, usually their sons. I did ease up on them, sometimes, as long as I was the starter. If the coaches played favorites and allowed their son or a friend's son to play ahead of me, I hit their sons so hard, that they refused to carry the ball while I was on the field. I was on the field for offense, defense, kick-off, kick-off return, and punt teams. That meant, eventually, their son was going to get hit, and hit hard. At some point in practice, I was going to win the starting position or injure their son's trying.

I felt justified hitting my coaches son's hard, because I had seen and experienced firsthand how some white coaches treated black players. I watched as superior black athletes got passed over for recognition, in favor of less talented white athletes. I hated racism, and I hated to lose even more. With every game we lost, I vowed to get better. If I suspected unfair treatment, their sons were going to pay the cost; even it meant that I had to run extra laps after practice or got benched during games.

While I liked hitting people, my greatest love was playing running back. I loved watching Gale Sayers carry the football for the Chicago Bears. He was fast, could stop on a dime, and made defenders miss tackles badly in the open field. He could change directions on a dime, and accelerate better than any football player I had ever seen.

I practiced his moves in the dirt, on black top, on gravel in the alley, and finally on the football field. One game, I scored six touchdowns and we still lost. Every time I crossed the end zone, I didn't have a dance. I bent down, while still in stride, and placed the ball on the ground. I wanted to give the impression that I had been there before and that it was no big deal to score. I wanted scoring touchdowns to look easy.

I had plenty of speed, but I had to learn how to go from zero to fast, stop on a dime, and accelerate, if I was going to become as important to my team, as Sayers' was to his. To increase my speed, I focused on track and field. I was inspired when I saw Tommie Smith and John Carlos raise their black-gloved fists, high into the air, after they placed first and second in the 100-meter dash at the Olympics in Mexico City.

My dad loved to watch the Olympics, but he was upset when those two athletes gave the sign for black power as they represented of our country on the podium. I thought what they did was pretty cool, and thrust my fist in the air to support them. Track and field was one of my favorite sports, and I could appreciate what they did, and why they did it.

I read about how track athletes exercised to increase their speed, and I mastered the technique of going from zero to fast. Soon, I realized that my extra work doing track exercises helped me develop another gear. I called it, "the passing gear." When most of my friends hit top speed, I realized that I could accelerate, even after hitting what used to be my top speed. I noticed that I could pull away from my competition, and I got into the habit of shutting it down before I crossed the finish line. This cockiness made my dad angry; but I did it anyway. From 1968 thru 1970, I had an uninterrupted winning streak in every track and field day event that I entered. I broke all of my older brother's records and was on my way to becoming the best athlete at my school.

PART III

DESPAIR AND MY TEENAGE YEARS

CHAPTER 5

DESPAIR

B y 1969, I was nine years old and I could sense that my older sisters and brothers were giving up hope that things would get better at home. My sisters were getting older, and I could hear them arguing trying to protect themselves from abuse. Since all the boys were in the basement, what I know for sure was that our abuse continued, unabated. Joe stayed away from home more and more, Rich stayed out later and later, and Clarence and I continued to fight.

Joe was my dad's namesake, but my dad liked Rich. One of the few times that I remembered Rich getting whipped was when he let Clarence and me go to the drive inn with him and his friends Butch, Donald, and Donnalee. We snuck out the window, which we all did on a regular basis, but this time, we stayed out all night watching five Clint Eastwood movies at the drive inn. When we got home, my dad was waiting, and he was fuming.

First, he took off his well worn black leather belt and beat Rich. Rich refused to make a sound, and held back tears because he didn't want to give my dad the satisfaction of making him cry. Clarence tried to be strong and hold his tears too, but he gave up after getting beat for about five minutes. Me, I was crying watching my brothers get whipped. When it was my turn, I tried to defend myself by grabbing his belt and running circles around him. I could never understand where the honor was, in just standing there and taking a beating.

Later that summer, Rich, Clarence and I were playing in the foothills and we noticed that a builder had discarded some usable lumber, sheet rock, and used doors. We carried the building materials home, and finished the basement. We put up walls, doors, and even managed to install working doorknobs that locked from the inside.

When our dad came down stairs to see what we had done, the sight of our work, which was done without the use of finishing materials, brought a smile to his face. We didn't know if he was pleased with our work, or if he was laughing at us on the inside. We suspected the latter because he framed the basement a long time ago, but never finished the job. Our running joke was to call him, "amma, amma, amma" behind his back, because he was always saying, "amma gonna" do this or "amma gonna" do that. He seldom got around to actually doing any of the things he promised. Now we had walls to separate the rooms that we shared, and we even got some privacy from each other every once in a while.

MOM AND BREAST CANCER

In 1970, my mom delivered the most devastating news of my life. Her doctor told her that she had breast cancer and wasn't expected to live. Dozens of thoughts raced through my mind. How could God take away the one person who believed in me? She was my security. I wasn't old enough to turn pro. How could I buy my mom the house that I promised her if she was dead? I went into my secret place, a crawl space in the basement, and cried my eyes out. I prayed to God to spare my mother's life. My mom was a strong women, and she was the source of my strength. I needed her.

My mom went into the hospital for surgery. Before she did, she squeezed my hand and told me that "momma's gonna be all right." I hoped and prayed that God would answer this one last prayer. I felt sad, betrayed and alone, but I continued to have hope.

The following Sunday, I went to church to say a special prayer for my mom. On most Sundays, I usually sat in the balcony, but not this time. This time, I walked to the front of the church, and sat alongside the white congregation. I worshiped God right alongside them. If God could raise Jesus from the dead, and part the Red Sea to save the Hebrews, surely he could spare my mom's life.

The doctors removed my mother's cancer, along with part of her breast, and ordered her to quit smoking cigarettes. I pledged to help her quit, one-half a cigarette at a time. I opened every pack of cigarettes that she owned, and drew a red line around it marking the place where she had to stop smoking and put the cigarette out. I checked every ashtray in the house every day, and if her brand of cigarette was more than half smoked, I demanded an explanation. I thought it was up to me to help our mother quit smoking; after all, God had answered my prayers, again.

At first, my mom thought the line I drew on the cigarettes was cute; however, she underestimated my resolve. Pack after pack, carton after carton, I took out cigarettes and marked them. If they were smoked past the red line, by my own hand, I enforced my will, just like she taught me. I cut full cigarettes in half and put half a cigarette back in the pack. Our mother was not amused. She tried hiding her cigarettes from me. I found them, and cut them in half. She threatened me, to no avail. She pleaded with me to stop cutting her cigarettes in half, but I refused to give in. She had to stop smoking, or else. Eventually, she did stop smoking. I had won. In reality, we all won. She beat cancer and cheated death, just like I did. When I told her that, she smiled and told me that she was gonna live a long time.

ABUSE AND THE DIVORCE

By 1972, I was twelve years old, and all hell broke loose in our house. My mom called a family meeting to tell us that she was divorcing my dad, and leaving home because he sexually abused some of her daughters. My dad admitted that he was wrong, and apologized to the family. I was angry, confused, shocked and dismayed by my dad's admission. All of my older brothers and sisters were either silent or crying.

I didn't really know why my dad came forward and told us the truth, but one of my older sisters told me that someone threatened to call the police on my dad and turn him in if he didn't confess. Knowing him, I don't believe that he would have come forward on his own, so I believed her.

By this time, my two older sisters had already moved out of the house, and my oldest brother Joe and older sister Zelna had enrolled in college at the University of Colorado at Boulder. Those of us who still lived at home were in disbelief. I remember several of us called my sister a liar, and sided with my dad. I knew that my dad abused us; but I still loved him and felt a need to protect him in his moment of weakness. My sister deserved our support, but it was close to impossible for a 12 year-old to believe that his father could have sex with his own daughter. At the end of the day, reconciliation was not an option and my parents divorced.

My mom went to Chicago to spend time with her brother, my uncle Clarence, and to clear her head. After a few weeks, she returned and dropped another bomb shell on us. She told me and Debbie that she was moving to Chicago, and was taking us with her. I didn't find out until I was much older that she whisked us away without telling my dad, even after she had agreed to give him custody of us in the divorce.

Debbie and I were afraid to move to Chicago. We had heard all the stories about how big the city was and how it was a dangerous place to live. I tried to put a brave face on, because I was really angry at my dad for all the years of abuse that he inflicted on us. But deep down inside, I couldn't get used to the idea that I would be leaving my older brothers and sisters behind. Rich and Barbara had taken care of us for much of our lives, and I loved them just as much as I loved my parents. In the end, my mom won out and we packed our bags and left for Chicago.

Life in Chicago

When we got to Chicago, we soon learned what big city life was all about. My mom had moved into a run-down, inner city apartment, with a man that she claimed to have known for years, she called Briddy. The apartment was small, we didn't have our own rooms to sleep in, but we had shelter.

My sister Debbie and I hooked up with our cousin Craig, our Uncle Clarence's son. Craig knew the streets on the Westside of Chicago and told us that we didn't go outside to play in Chicago. In fact, when we went to our Uncle's house, several blocks away, Craig told me that there were three run-zones along the way. As Craig explained it, a run-zone was a neighborhood where you had to run to get through it safely. As long as we were running, the gangs who controlled that turf might let us pass through their territories without hurting us. This was my first taste of big city life. Moving from a sleepy little town in Colorado to inner city Chicago was no small adjustment.

One morning, we were running through a gang neighborhood and were not so lucky. A couple of teenage gang members spotted us running through their hood and demanded money from us. My little sister and I didn't have a dime between us, and my cousin wasn't about to pay a dime to get through. When one of the gang members pulled a knife, Craig spotted a small, three-legged bar-b-que grill on a nearby porch. Craig and I made eye contact and made a dash for the grill. My cousin grabbed the grill and smashed it on the ground. He took a leg, I took a leg and the fight was on.

After we defended ourselves with the grill legs, the gang retreated to call in re-enforcements. We wasted no time and resumed our run, cutting through laundry-mats, barbershops and restaurants, front to back, until we were clear of their territory. Neighborhood gangs respected other gang's territories and let us go after we got off their turf.

The second run zone had a vicious junkyard dog that could get underneath his fence. It looked like a mutt, black with brown spots, and was mixed with pure mean. It was muscular too, and it slobbered white foam from its angry jaws. The trick was for us to run past the hole in the fence and allow the dog to chase us, before it realized that it had to run back to its hole in the fence, climb through, and resume chase on our side of the fence. By the time the dog caught up, we were on the other side of the street and it was trained not to cross the street. It pranced back to its hole in the fence, satisfied that it did its job, and waited for other potential victims. That dog had a reputation because it killed a person.

The third run zone was a string of nightclubs where dangerous thugs, pimps and criminals hung out day and night. Someone was always having a bad day, and waited for young boys like my cousin and me to pass by so they could take our money, clothes, or make us run drugs for them in plain view of the Chicago PD. Most of those men were armed and extremely dangerous.

One night, we were walking home and passed through an alley behind a nightclub where we saw Chicago's finest taking payments at the backdoor, while crimes were being committed at the front. Just as we made it to Michigan Avenue, we heard some men talking about a man who got chased from the club, crossed the street and tried to hide underneath a Buick Electra 225, or what was better known in Chicago as a deuce-and-a-quarter. The man chasing him, crossed the street as well, bent down and fired what they said looked like a nine-millimeter, semiautomatic pistol, underneath the car killing him. No one saw a thing that night, no witnesses. We continued on our way, only to hear three other men talking about a man making a call in a phone booth get gunned down by killers driving a deuce-and-a-quarter. All of them knew whose car it was, but none of them saw a thing. Debbie stayed at my Uncle's house that night, and Craig and I were happy that we made it home safely.

The next morning, we learned that Debbie and our aunt were not so lucky. My uncle was always wheeling and dealing and he associated with shady characters. This time, he was away from home when some thugs he crossed paid a visit to his home. They found my sister and aunt, tied them up with duck tape, and robbed his home. They also stripped down his fully loaded Cadillac, left it on bricks, and painted no-radio on the side. They could have wrote, no seats, no spare tire, and no TV antenna. My sister and aunt were lucky the thugs spared their lives.

All the time I spent in Chicago was not bad. We got ice cream, the cars people drove were shiny and new, and people dressed to kill. I picked up a few stylish pieces that were a hit when I got back to the Springs. I got a nice pair of blue and green plaid baggies and a blue-green shirt to go with it. New clothes! Until that time, the only new cloths I got were for Easter or Christmas. Otherwise, I got hand-me-downs that didn't fit my older brothers. Usually, my mom sewed up the holes and took in the waist so much that my pants could have fit snugly on a skeleton.

After my second week in Chicago, I learned to cuss, pay attention to my surroundings, and that life could be over in a moments' notice. Neighborhood gangs would attack anyone for crossing the street. People we didn't know would attack us to pay back my uncle. And sometimes, Chicago's finest just looked the other way.

Later in the week, my brother Joe made his way to Chicago and found where we lived. He brought a message from my dad. He made sure that we understood that our dad killed many people in Korea, and was planning a trip to Chicago to kill us if we didn't return home with him. After learning about what my dad did to my sisters, there was no doubt in my mind that he was capable of doing just about anything.

Joe understood his role in our family; he was our dad's enforcer. He led the attack on our sister's credibility, and was our dad's staunchest defender. Besides that, I believed what he said about my dad. My dad knew his way around Chicago, and it seemed like the killers got away clean. I went home with him and Debbie stayed behind for a few more days before returning home.

After this brief hiatus in Chicago, I was back living with my dad who tried even harder to break my spirit. He continued to gamble away his money, and he continued to try to impose his will on me. In my mind, his imposing his will on me days were over. I knew his dirty little secret and lost respect for him, as a man. To me, he was lower than pond scum. All that was left was for him to do was to find more creative ways to control me, and for me to get old enough to do for myself.

DRUGS, ALCOHOL AND PUBERTY

In the fall, I was fourteen years old, and I enrolled at Holmes Junior High school. The stress in my life began to take its toll on me. I had a front row seat when my mom survived breast cancer. I saw a strong and vibrant woman, becoming frail and sickly, and in our house, weakness was a punishable crime. I saw the pain in her face when my sisters forced my dad to admit incest. I also experienced her divorce from my dad after she gave up custody, and still tried to take her last two children from a man who she knew was abusing us. I felt my mom's pain as if it were my own. To escape the pain I felt inside, I experimented with drugs and alcohol.

First, it was alcohol. My friend Tom met me at the bus stop with a baby food jar full of whisky. We shared it before going on to school. By the time I got to school, I was feeling like nothing mattered. Under the influence of alcohol, I was even more cocky, talked to older girls, and made plans to rendezvous at isolated places on schools grounds. Most of the time, we held hands, kissed and talked about our parents. It seemed like all of our parents were intolerable jerks. We made plans for the weekend.

On the weekend, the district opened up my old grade school for teen nights. They were trying to find structured, nighttime activities for us, to keep us off the streets and out of trouble. My friends and I arrived with several baby food jars full of whisky, and lots of energy. Sometimes the girl I wanted to see would be there, sometimes not, but there was never a shortage of willing girls whose hormones were as raging out of control as mine. More kissing and talking before the night would be over and my friends and I met up to compare notes. We had the usual stories, my girl was fine, Terry had a younger girl and spent the night trying to persuade her to kiss him, and my other friend Eddie, he had the fat girl.

During the week at school, I generally misbehaved. Lunchtime was always a challenge. I never had lunch money. If I was lucky, breakfast was one of those miniature boxes of cereal, sometimes with milk, most of the time dry or with water. At school, I asked to use the restroom and roamed the halls checking for open lockers. You would be surprised how many students left their lockers unlocked. I rummaged through their lunch bags, lifted a few items, and ate the food right away. There was never anything worth stealing in my locker, but I made sure it was locked tight.

After school, I had football practice. This was often the best part of my day. I padded up, strapped on my helmet and took my pent up frustration out on unsuspecting kids who didn't know me. I played running back on offense and safety on defense. With my speed and quickness, I scored at will against my teammates and often against my opponents at game-time as well. On defense, I tried my best to separate the ball carrier from the ball.

Most of the time, my coached liked the fact that I practiced as hard as I played in real games, unless I was hitting their sons. They praised me and rewarded me by making me a team captain every year that I played. In practice, and in games, I called at least one safety blitz. I called the blitz because it allowed me get running start from my safety position, twelve yards behind the line of scrimmage, and try to anticipate the snap count. Whether I timed the snap count right or not, the result was same, with one small detail. If I guessed right, I passed through the offensive line like a knife cutting through warm butter, and I drilled the quarterback into the ground before he knew what hit him. If I guessed wrong, same result; however, I got called for a five yard penalty, but those were only in games. Penalty or not, the quarterbacks I played against knew I was coming and often made mistakes when they saw me moving towards the line of scrimmage. In games or in practice, the quarterbacks knew that they were about to feel the pain. All that mattered to me was that, on defense, I wanted to hit somebody hard, every play, and on offense, I wanted the ball in my hands.

After a long day of school and practice, I usually went home to a house that was full of strife. My dad would be home, usually watching TV and smoking Old Golds. Most of the time, there would be a left over pork chop and few shriveled up green beans that no one wanted. Sometimes, there would be no dinner at all, and he would come home late after gambling away his paycheck or drinking with his buddies. On those days, I went to bed tired and hungry.

When spring rolled around, it was track season. I always liked track and field. It gave me an opportunity to display my speed and jumping ability, and more importantly, it allowed me to regain a sense of purpose and control in my life. It also allowed me to meet girls from other schools at track meets at their schools.

Still in seventh grade, I lost my first race ever to a white boy. Until this race, I dominated the white athletes at my school. In my mind, black athletes were superior to white athletes, and the races were over before they began. My psychological superiority came crashing down when my friend Tim beat me in the 100-yard dash. I couldn't believe it. We were neck and neck for about 50 yards, where I usually turned on the after burners and pulled away from the competition. Many times, I had a big enough lead to shut it down just before crossing the finish line. It didn't happen, I turned on the jets and Tim pulled away from me. I stumbled trying to catch him.

Tim and I became close friends and he introduced me to smoking weed. He smoked cigarettes and pot, and ran faster than a gazelle. He had long, dirty brown hair, and came from a family that was pretty well to do. I tried smoking pot too, coughed a lot when I inhaled, and got stoned. Now I was drinking before school and smoking pot at school. I was never a very good student, except in math, but after taking a few swigs of whisky and smoking pot, I couldn't remember any of the lessons that I went to school to learn.

By eighth grade, our dad lost the house. He told me later that he let the house go, without selling it, because he didn't want our mom to get a dime from the sale. I didn't know whether to believe him or not. He may have told me that to cover up the fact that he couldn't manage his money. My mom had given him twenty years of marriage, and seven children. She raised nine of us, and ran the household on the money he provided, as best she could. Certainly, that was worth something. But not to my dad, that is, if he was telling me the truth.

When we moved out of our home, our dad arranged for Clarence, Rich and me to live with his best friend, who was a decorated Colonel. None of us really knew the Colonel, but he took us in and provided some army cots for us to sleep on in his basement. He told us that the spare key to his house was in the keyo on the ledge of his house, and that we could let ourselves in. None of us knew what a keyo was, so there we were, three, black, teenage boys, walking around a white Colonel's house looking for a key in a keyo so we could let ourselves in. We were lucky no one called the police on us. After looking for several minutes, we finally found the key hidden inside of a sprinkler in on the ledge, and went inside. Had it not been for the Colonel's generosity, we would have been homeless.

My sister Barbara went to live with our sister Zelna and Debbie lived with my dad's girlfriend, for a short time. My brothers and I were separated from our sisters until my dad rented a house on the North part of town on Villa Circle. When we moved into the house, we were all happy to be back together and to have a place to live in again.

Debbie and I enrolled at Russell Junior High, Debbie in seventh grade and me in eighth. Clarence enrolled at Palmer High School, and Barbara finished her senior year at Coronado. Rich lived with us too, and attended college at Colorado College for a short time before he quit and enrolled at Pikes Peak Community College.

From what I could tell, Rich and Barbara had changed. Barbara lived in a constant state of depression. One can only imagine how she must have felt, still living in the same house with an abusive dad. When she was home, a smile never found her face. There was no way for us to know the pain she had endured. She had endured so much abuse, that she kind of gave up on living.

She told me later on in life that by the time she graduated from high school and moved to Boulder Colorado to attend Colorado University that psychologically, she wasn't able to adjust to college life and dropped out. Her quitting college was a tragedy because she truly was a brilliant scholar, an outstanding athlete and was the most caring person in our family.

Rich changed too. I remember him getting an F in high school. No one in our family had ever gotten an F before. Rich went from being the guy who would surpass your best efforts in most sports, or out think you, to a guy who would tear down our accomplishments to boost his fragile self-esteem. Somewhere along the way, he went from being an extroverted leader, to an introverted loner.

Rich told me later on in life that he dropped out of Colorado College because my dad tried to control him, even after he was in college, and I believed him. But there was another reason too. Rich was a good athlete, but when he enrolled in CC, he ran into all state athletes, Terry Miller and Ronald June. Those brothas were the fastest people in the state and they had beaten him time after time in the Junior Olympics. Psychologically, I think he needed to get away from my dad. He eventually enrolled at CU, got married, and dropped out of college.

CHAPTER 6

LIVING IN THE SHADOW OF WEALTH

Time will tell what affect this period of our lives had on Clarence, Debbie and me. We all went to new schools, lived in a new neighborhood, and made new friends. Many of the kids at Russell were better off financially than our friends at Holmes. Several of my friends lived in million dollar homes, high on the cliffs that overlooked the valley where we lived. Two of my friends Stewart and Andy both had pools and three or four fireplaces in their homes. One of my friends dad owned part of the business that made those miniature rockets that kids liked to assemble and blast off into space.

For fun, they had motorcycles and snowmobiles. They skiied every weekend during the winter months, and always had nice clothes and down-filled jackets to wear. One day it snowed real bad and a helicopter landed in front of the school and picked up Andy and Stewart.

For the most part, our lives were in disarray and very stressful. On the surface, we had a home to live in and we were glad for that. However, there was still very little money to go around and many times, to many to count; we stared across the kitchen table at each other, hoping against hope that we would actually have something to eat.

At school, I tried wrestling. My other brothers had done it and had some success, so I gave it a try. I stunk at it. I hated the practices and the matches. Many of the other athletes had been wrestling for years and knew lots of techniques that they used to control me on the mat. All the moves that I knew, were either illegal or didn't work against experienced wrestlers. During matches, they pinned me to the mat and I couldn't even throw any punches.

I prayed a lot. I missed my old friends and wanted to feel normal, if just for a moment. I began to realize that I had to leave childlike thoughts behind. I was becoming a young man, and with that understanding, I began to accept reality as it came. Fighting everybody and everything, everyday, just wasn't a solution to my problems.

The time came for me to shift gears. This time when I downshifted, it wasn't on the track, it was in my mind. Seeing Barbara's pain, even depression, every day and watching Rich give up, let me know that I had better think-through my decisions and not just think about them after I made them.

BACK ON HOME TURF

By the ninth grade, I was fifteen years old, and we were on the move again. My dad couldn't pay the rent and the landlord kicked us out. This time, we moved into the Blue Fox motel, in the Red Light district, on North Nevada Avenue, five miles from downtown Colorado Springs. The brick, strip-mall type, structure was painted sky blue and trimmed in white. That color scheme made it standout to travelers who intended to pass through Colorado Springs on Highway 85-87.

The rooms were tiny, with dingy white, paper thin walls that looked as if they had not been painted in decades. The mattress on the bed was lumpy and the red carpet on the floor was stained with who knows what. At night when I should have been sleeping, I could hear prostitutes turning tricks all night long. Every hour or so, I could hear men moaning with excitement and the hookers egging them on. As I lay in my bed, happy for a place to rest my head, all I could think about was why my dad took his own daughters. I resented him for what he'd done and wanted to lash out at him, but for now, he was safe. For food, we were basically on our own. Lucky for us, we qualified for free lunch at school.

When we tried to enroll in our old schools, the receptionist wanted to know our address. Of course, none of us knew it. We were back to telling school officials that we lived on Nevada Avenue and they could call our dad for the address. We weren't homeless, but I was still embarrassed when my friends asked where I lived. Debbie and I hooked up with our old friends, which meant drinking before school, smoking cigarettes or pot at school, and practice after school. My friends usually supplied the weed and alcohol.

GOD'S PERFECT TIMING

HIGH SCHOOL

Nineteen seventy five, I made it to High School at Coronado. My older brother Clarence was in the 12th grade and I was in the 10th. The year started with a teachers strike and the district hired substitute teachers. The students supported the teachers and we ditched classes until our regular teachers came back. I was never a very good student, and took advantage of the teacher strike as an excuse for achieving poor academic marks.

My friends usually had a few dollars in their pockets and bought food and something to drink from the cafeteria that we took out to the striking teachers. This was against the rules, but no one, especially me was keen on following the rules anyway.

In class, it was total chaos. Substitute teachers didn't have lesson plans, and students were in no mood to cooperate. Only the A students stayed in class and tried to learn something. The rest of us generally helped our teachers disrupt the education process. We showed up in class without books, claimed that we were no assigned homework, and pulled the fire alarm, multiple times.

I can't remember how long the strike lasted, but the district eventually gave in to the teachers' demands. When school got underway, high school was fun. Just like going from elementary school to junior high school, there were more people. Like all of my friends, I had to make the transition from being the oldest students at the school, to the youngest.

My first semester in high school, Laura caught my eye. She was a Junior, who was dating one of my brother's friends Steve, who was a Senior. Laura was a white girl, not overly attractive, but she was pretty, had a nice personality and nice figure. Steve was a Mexican, about Clarence's size. For some reason, Steve beat Laura up all the time. Day after day, Laura came to school with black eyes.

One day I saw her crying in the smoking area at school and asked her what happened. She told me that Steve had beaten her up, again. I confronted Steve and asked him why he kept beating her up. He replied, "That's none of you business." He was right of course, but I had no shortage of testosterone, and I told him that it would be better if he quit hitting her. He asked me what I was going to do about it if he didn't. Steve may have been friends with my brother and he may have been a senior, but that was the wrong answer. I challenged Steve to meet me after school. He agreed.

Steve told Clarence that I called him out, but that he wouldn't fight me if Clarence was going to jump in. By now, Clarence had developed a reputation for beating up older boys who picked on me for one reason or another. Clarence told him that it probably wasn't a good idea to fight me, but that he wouldn't jump in. Steve had all the reassurance he needed to meet me after school, and he did.

After school, Steve showed up with Clarence and their other friends. The side of the school where we met was not visible from the street. Steve tried to talk, to reason with me, but I wasn't having any of it. Besides, I didn't come to talk, I came to fight. I swung on Steve with a left and he blocked it, but he couldn't get out of the way of my right and I clocked him in the nose with a straight right. Steve swung on me with a right and I blocked it and countered with a right hook to his gut. When I saw the air leaving his body, and him bending over, I grabbed his head and kneed him in the face. When he fell on his back, I jumped on top of him and delivered a combination of lightning quick blows to his face until my brother and his friends pulled me off him. My adrenaline was flowing, my heart was pounding, and I was just getting started. I tried to kick him when they pulled me off him.

When they let me go, I stood over Steve and told him that if he ever put his hands on Laura again, I'd kill him. I think he believed me because he never touched her again. In fact, he broke up with her. Clarence told me that Steve was afraid to hold her hand because he thought I would make good on my threat.

The next day when I saw Laura, she asked me what happened to Steve. Someone had beaten him up pretty bad. He had two black eyes, a cut lip and his face was red and swollen. Laura was concerned because he wouldn't even talk to her. At first I told her that I heard he ran into a wall. She looked puzzled, and I told her that Steve wouldn't be hitting her anymore. Laura knew that Steve and my brother were friends and asked if I got Clarence and his friends to beat Steve up. I told her no, that I called him out and he accepted. She cried and told me that no one ever stood up for her before. She kissed me, I kissed her back, and we started seeing each other.

People heard about the fight, and it earned me the right to roam the hallways with a swagger. I was seeing an older girl, and Clarence was there just in case.

Not too many kids in the school wanted any part of Clarence or his friends Felix and Byron. Felix was around 6-foot tall, medium build, and his dad owned a construction company. Byron was a big brotha, a year younger than Clarence, but had two older brothers, Everett and Lydell, that had gone to Coronado. His brother's reputations were legendary. One year, during football season, Everett and Lydell walked on the football field and called out the entire football team. There were no takers. Those brothers would seriously hurt you, if you even thought about hurting any of their family or friends.

In class, all the teachers thought they knew me. Four of my older brothers and sisters went to Coronado. When they called my name off the class roster, all I heard was, "Another Caruth? How many of you Caruth's are there? Are there any more?" Actually, there was, Debbie was on her way. They rattled off my brothers and sisters names, Zelna, Richard, Barbara, Clarence. The class thought it was funny; I wasn't amused, I had heard this story at every school I went to, except for Russell.

In Chemistry, the teacher stopped class and told us a story about how Rich blew up the chemistry lab. Oh, he went into detail about how my brother and is friend Donnalee, were conducting an experiment with urine and blew up the whole lab, urine flew everywhere. By now, I had grown weary of being compared to my older brothers and sisters. The only source of comfort that I had was that my friend Herral, who was sitting there next to me, his brother, was also involved in the explosion. Herral and I just wanted to learn chemistry; I just wanted to pass the class if I could.

After school, I had football practice. The players got out of class a few minutes earlier than the other students so that we could change into our uniforms. In the locker room, the upperclassmen had a practice of initiating the sophomores. Generally, they picked on the weaker guys first. They had a way of rolling the towels so that they wouldn't come unwrapped when they snapped them. They also wet the tip with a little water so it would sting a little more when they popped the sophomores with them.

Most of the players who got initiated first were white boys. Many of them had never been in a fight in their lives, and had played little league with their coach dads who protected them. I resented them because most of them were weaker than the black players, but their dads made up for their deficiencies with preferential treatment and coaching clinics. My dad never took the time to coach me, so I never had that problem of getting to play because my dad was coach. I earned playing time, and didn't mind getting out there and mixing it up with the big boys.

In the locker room it was like a turkey shoot. Young, skinny white boys and even the bigger ones got popped on their butts and legs with towels. Their white legs turned red and welled-up in a matter seconds. Some of them got popped in the groin area and they fell to the ground in pain. All the while, the upperclassmen laughed and had a good time. I had taken so many whippings that I was glad to see someone else, anyone else, getting tortured.

When they got to me, I wasn't having it. I had whipped a senior earlier in the year and they also knew that most of the black players would fight before we accepted being tortured, and I was no exception. I knew that I had older brothers who would back me up if I needed, and they knew it too. I escaped their torture ritual.

1976 THE JIMMY CARTER YEARS

Clarence moved on to attend college at CU Boulder, and Debbie joined me at Coronado. Debbie and I shared some of the same frustrations with our dad. During this time in our lives, he was a working as a Maytag repairman. It pained him to have to do repairman work after his military career, but he manned up and did what he had to do to put a roof over our heads.

Adjusting to his new line of work was not easy, and he took his frustrations out on us. To wash our clothes, in the coin-operated laundry room that had Maytag washers and dryers that my dad repaired, he gave us enough change for one load. To wash all of our clothes, we learned how to cheat the machine by pushing the coins in very slowly; listening for clicks that started the machines, and then pulling the coins back out before they were deposited into the coin receptacle. We got quite good at cheating the washing machines, but the few times that we were not successful and the machines kept the change, my dad refused to give us more coins. We had to recycle dirty clothes, or scrounge around the house looking under sofa cushions for spare change, or simply let our clothes mildew or dry on their own.

To make matters worse, my dad was a chain smoker and filled several ashtrays with cigarette butts. He expected Debbie and me to clean up after him, and to keep his ashtrays clean. If we were working on homework or minding our own business, he called us to empty the ashtrays, while he rested his feet on the coffee table and smoked. I think he thought we were his slaves, not his children.

The following summer, I called Clarence, who was attending college at CU Boulder. I told him that I had to get away from dad before something bad happened. I explained that dad was trying to treat me like a slave and that we were going to exchange blows very soon. Clarence had a better relationship with my dad than I did. He also knew that I was serious, had studied martial arts, and that I wasn't afraid. He told me to hold tight and invited me to spend the summer with him in Boulder. Clarence hopped in his car and drove to the Springs. I packed up a few clothes, and I spent the summer with him in Boulder.

THE SUMMER IN BOULDER THAT SAVED MY LIFE

The University of Colorado at Boulder is nestled at the base of the Rocky Mountains, about twenty miles west of Denver. The campus was spacious, beautiful and full of life. Clarence lived in a little apartment with his girlfriend Paula. While attending school, he also worked at King Suppers, to pay his way through college. He told me that when dad took him to college, he dropped him and his trunk full of belongings off at a bus stop just within the Boulder city limits, gave him ten bucks, told him good luck, and drove away. He caught the bus to campus, trunk in tow, and went through the registration process by himself.

Clarence stayed in the dorm his first year and moved off campus to a little apartment where he lived the second year. His apartment was nice. He had a big fish tank with two pet Oscars in it. Those fish were bigger than normal gold fish that you usually saw in people's homes. He also had to buy mill worms to feed them.

He had a nice stereo sound system, with four-feet tall speakers, and a T.V. that sat on a make shift wall unit made up of bricks and particle boards. He had the latest albums, food in his fridge and he was excelling in school. He gave me a key to his pad, and showed me around town. I learned where he worked and explored campus.

My stay in Bounder was fun. I walked around campus, met college girls, and went to parties. There were lots of freshmen on campus who weren't much older than me. I lied to them about my age and told them that I was about to enroll in college too, but that I was just checking CU out to see if I wanted to go there. They did their best to convince me that Boulder was the place to be. They showed me around campus, their favorite partying spots on the Hill, and invited me to parties around campus. I could see why all of my older brothers and sisters went to CU for college. Life in Boulder was exciting. It was so exciting, none of them graduated.

I also learned that Clarence was no choirboy. He hung with a pretty rough crowd, mixed in with the drug culture and generally had a chip on his shoulder. During the day, he was a mild mannered college student with girlfriend and a job. At night, he was a smalltime drug dealer who socialized with common street thugs from Denver. He usually kept small amounts of weed in his apartment for personal use and I helped myself to a joint or two every now and then. He didn't mind, and he made sure that I always had a few bucks in my pocket.

Clarence had a steady girlfriend, Paula. She was petite, very attractive, had a Coke bottle body, and shared his apartment with him. I also learned that she had sisters, at least two that I met, and they were fine too. One evening, Clarence arranged for a double date with him and Paula, and Paula's sister Sharon and me. Clarence drove to their house so that we could pick up her sister and we waited inside until Sharon got ready. While we waited for Sharon to get ready, her other sister Jackie walked out of the bathroom, buck naked, and walked down the hall to her room in the direction where I was sitting. We made eye contact and she made it clear that she wanted me to see all that she had to offer. I saw it all right, and I liked what I saw too. That sista was fine.

We all went out that evening. Clarence had sprung for some concert tickets and we were going to have a great time. In route to the concert, Paula had noticed that Sharon and I were getting a little too cozy for her liking in the back seat and tried to run interference by asking how we were doing. I should have kept it simple and said fine, and went back to kissing her sister. But, I had to add a little extra by saying that Jackie and I were fine. My night may have well of ended right then. Sharon pulled away and got an attitude. I had committed an unforgivable sin; I called her by her sisters' name. The truth of the matter was that, subconsciously, I couldn't get the nude image of her sister Jackie out of my mind. I got no more kisses that night and my date was as cool as ice.

I went back to the Springs after having gotten a taste of college life. I learned the latest dances, discovered new music, and most of all; I had a chance to get away from my dad. He was the same when I got back, but I was a little better prepared to deal with him. I knew college was in my future, and that I only had to tolerate living with my dad for one more year.

Looking back, my stay in Boulder that summer probably saved my life, or my dad's. Either way, my life would have changed forever had I stayed in the Springs. I was maturing into a young man and hated my dad. I found myself thinking about ways I could hurt him, knowing all along, that my dad was a big man who had killed before if I failed. God had other plans for me.

PART IV

STRUCK BY LIGHTNING

CHAPTER 7

THE GATE OF HEAVEN

My getting struck by lightning was no accident of nature. I challenged God to prove to me that he really existed. One week later, I received God's answer to my prayer and I didn't have to like it. For me, death was preferable to a life with no chance of playing big-time college football and eventually playing in the NFL. When the lightning struck, my spirit tried to accept death, but God had other plans for me.

David Caruth, holding up sox I was wearing when I got struck by lightning, 1977.

Coronado High School student and football player David Caruth holds up the socks he wore when he was struck by lightning on August 18.

Just as God directed his lightning, he directed my spirit to reenter my body. My spirit was obedient and the transformation from the person I was, to the person God wanted me to become, had begun. I had to live life as me again, with all of my old problems and some new ones. The new ones were more troublesome than I ever could have imagined, and they are permanent.

When I regained awareness from the coma in my hospital bed, in the physical sense, I realized that while I was in the spiritual world, I didn't have a body, just an awareness that allowed understanding. I needed something good to happen, in the physical world, to take my mind off my injuries, when Rissa, stopped by to see me.

I liked Rissa. She was strikingly beautiful, had long hair, a coco brown complexion, a Coke bottle figure, and pleasant personality. Whenever I saw her, her beauty made me smile. She leaned over to give me a kiss, you know, the kind you get from your mother, but I wasn't having any of that. Within seconds, our tongues were swirling around in each other's mouths. Rissa had full, luscious lips that were often covered with flavored lip-gloss. Kissing her always tasted good.

The next few days, I spent learning how to walk. A physical therapist came in to assist me, and my first steps reminded me of my childhood in Arizona when I first learned how to walk with the orthopedic shoes that had the bar that connected my feet. Only this time, it was different. I was taller and the therapist had to hold on to a badly burned body. My charred skin had begun to heal and every movement hurt because my skin lacked its normal elasticity and scabs had begun to form all over my body. My brain had to order my leg to take a step because it was too painful for my legs to take steps on their own. The therapist had to hold me up because I had no balance and couldn't stand under my own power. I grimaced in pain with each step I took, and each step required a separate order from my brain. By the time my therapy for the day was over, I was exhausted both mentally and physically.

By my seventh and eighth days in the hospital, my friends and other relatives stopped by to see me. They all wanted to know how I was doing. What they found was me starting rehab and walking with considerable difficulty and pain. I still couldn't hear very well, but at least now, I understood why. My ears felt like someone stuck ice picks in them and turned them in corkscrew fashion to intensify the affect. The pain in my ears was so intense, that pain medicine did little to ease the discomfort of an itch that I couldn't scratch. No matter, I was glad to see my friends. My friends made me laugh and reminded me that I still had them, even though, deep down in my soul, I was depressed because I knew that my dream of playing professional football was lost forever.

When I entered the hospital, I weighed 165 pounds. Eighteen days later, I left the hospital weighing 112. As I was being wheeled out of the hospital in a wheelchair, I saw the nurse whose jaw I had broken after coming out of my coma. Her jaw was wired shut and she was not pleased to see me. I tried to offer her my most heartfelt apology, but she wouldn't accept it. Her coming in contact with me changed her life forever, and I deeply regret that fact. I prayed for her forgiveness.

Little did I know, from the moment I got struck by lightning on, people I came in contact with would be interacting with someone whose life should have ended. Some would grow to hate me, because I ignored the power that they assumed they had in the physical world. It was impossible to tell everyone I met that they were free to bask in their ignorance of their very existence, at least for a moment, but that someday, they would meet death only to find that their spirit was subject to God's Will.

Some people would come to love me, even though I had committed a multitude of sins. It's a strange thing to have the core of your inner being changed in the blink of eye. On the one hand, I was changed, forever. On the other hand, I had to transition from the person I was, in the physical world, to the person God wanted me to become. My world was no longer black and white, nor was it a kaleidoscope of colors. Rather, it became multiple shades of grey, with thin, undistinguishable lines that separated right from wrong, good from bad, and love from hate.

At the same time, others who came in contact with me would be too engrossed in their own journeys to notice. Nonetheless, God made it clear to me during my spiritual experience that he had designs on my life. No longer could I plan to live my life bringing pain to people I came in contact with. I had to help them, at least some of them. Imagine that, me helping other people. God took my mom's most ignorant, disobedient and rebellious son, and transformed me into something I was not, someone who would help people for no other reason than they existed.

When I went back to high school that year, I was far behind in schoolwork. I never was a good student, like my other brothers and sisters. At best, I was a slow learner and below average student. I tried to resume a normal life, but now I was weak, slow, and had to help people. I knew for sure that God had the power to change my life, and now so do you. What I wasn't so sure of was how long it was going to take for him to change a person like me from the person I was to the person he wanted me to become.

One of the strangest things that happened to me when I crossed over from life to death was that I was at war when my spirit left my body and at peace when it returned. At that precise moment, I knew that I would have to overcome my fears and face head-on the consequences of my decisions, both good and bad, and take responsibility for the multitude of mistakes that I made that brought meaning to my life.

For years, I dreaded knowing that I had to write this book. I played a game of mental chess with myself, thinking five moves ahead, only to realize that my counter moves would be equally effective against my best strategy against writing this book. At the end of the game, I knew that I had to figure out how to put into words, that I challenged God to prove to me that he really existed and that he responded by hitting me with the largest bolt of lightning ever to hit a person who lived to tell about it.

What hurts the most is that I promised my mom that I would buy her a house after I signed a contract with a professional football team. My mom survived the death of both of her parents at a young age, helped raise her two younger sisters and younger brother on the streets of Chicago, raised nine children of her own, and survived cancer. She deserved to live out the rest of her days comfortably. How could I adjust to God taking away any chance I had to play professional football and provide a better life for my mom? How could he expect me to accept not becoming a professional athlete as a consequence of his proving to me that he existed? I had prepared my whole life to achieve success on the football field. I was mean, strong and prepared to use any means necessary to achieve my goal.

I can't count the number of times I asked myself if God could really change a person in the blink of an eye who had dedicated his life to hurting people to someone who would help people. Surely he must have known how difficult it would be for me to unlearn most of the bad habits I developed over the first seventeen years of my life. With my spirit exposed to the power and glory of God, and a badly damaged and charred body, I knew that I had no choice but to begin life anew.

The trouble with this anointing is that, in my neighborhood, it was still hurt or get hurt. I thought it was better to dish-out pain, rather than be on the receiving end. Certainly on the football field, where I was praised for hitting other players with a fierce reckless abandon, bringing as much pain to other players as I could, it should have been acceptable, even to God. On the field of play, God allows other men to ignore pain, and to slam into each other with as much force as their physical bodies can muster.

In exchange for taking my physical strength, I learned later on in life, that I received an inner strength that drove me to give voice to the voiceless or to stand firm in the face of injustice, even if I had to stand alone. God replaced my physical power with the courage to speak truth to power, even at the expense of my own immediate, personal gain, and sometimes at great cost. I can't tell you how many times I have asked God why He decided to change me the way He did. Even if I needed an attitude adjustment, couldn't He have allowed me to experience a more pleasant miracle instead of hitting me with a bolt of lightning?

To find answers to my inner thoughts, I searched the Holy Bible and here is what I found. Since my mom named me after David, that is where I began my quest for knowledge. In the Bible, David had to learn painful lessons along the way as he moved about his life to escape the wrath of Saul. What I learned is that following God's path has never been easy. Sometimes, many times, I strayed from his path and pursued my own. Following my own path led to my learning painful lessons, but I have grown from them. I also met good people along the way who have enriched my life and in some small way; I hope that I have enriched theirs.

I didn't know how long it would take for my transformation to be complete, or how I was going to be able to make a living that would allow me to buy a house for my mom. All I knew was that God put an anointing on my life, and that I had to help people, not hurt them. I also knew that I could pray to him for guidance, and that he would answer my prayers.

After I got struck by lightning, I started living life all over again, at age seventeen. I accepted the fact that my football playing days were over, so I ran track the second semester of my senior year at high school.

David Caruth running track, Coronado High School, 1978.

My speed wasn't what it was before the injury but I managed to compete. I ran the 100-yard dash; the 220-yard dash; long-jumped; triple-jumped, and ran the 4 X 100 yard relay. There were no college scouts interested in me, no chance for a scholarship to attend college, and an uncertain future awaited me. All I had to look forward to was finding a way to graduate and knowing that God had his own plans for me.

When I tried to gain knowledge that would help me understand my experience with death, I had nowhere to turn, except the Bible. I read about how God allowed David to take down Goliath, advise Kings, and then stripped him of all of his blessings until he had to rely on God. The one assurance that I had was that God protected David through all of his trials and tribulations and that he would protect me as well. The only problem was that God lets people learn from their mistakes, and that some of those lessons would be quite painful.

One lesson that I didn't expect was that, at seventeen years old, I had to depend on myself to monitor my recovery and to determine the severity and extent of any permanent neurological damage that resulted from the lightning. Neither of my parents seemed to grasp what my doctors told them regarding the permanent nature of my injuries. The doctors were convinced that I would never be the same because people who suffered the type of injuries that I did, and who were comatose as a result, often emerged from comas with a combination of physical, intellectual and memory problems that usually required special attention.

For many years, after my four days in a coma, I could not get a decent night's sleep. As I begin to enter deep REM sleep, subconsciously, my body recognized that I might be slipping back into a coma, my breathing pattern heightened and my brain forced my muscles to move. After about a minute of forcing myself to breath and move, I awaken from deep sleep and lay restless until it is time to get ready for the day's activities, whatever they may be. When one considers what happens to the human body after a few days of sleeplessness, it is a miracle that I have been able to string two good decisions together in a row, and find any sort of success at all.

Life after getting struck by lightning has been anything but easy, especially when God decides to teach you that His will, not your own, will have the dominant impact on the course of your life. Make no mistake, throughout my life, I chose which paths to follow, when to do right and when to do wrong, and who to hurt or help. What I didn't know, was that God would extract blessings from me, that I didn't earn, and give them to other people, sometimes to people I didn't even like, free of charge. At the same time, he would cause other people to cross paths with me on a day that it would take an act of God to get me to concede an inch.

Neither of my parents thought about how I was going to provide for my long-term care. I ended up scheduling my own surgery to repair my ruptured eardrums, five times, before doctors declared that it was safe for me to get water in my ears, or to go swimming. I struggled to hear normal speech, without hearing aids, throughout my senior year in high school.

I also suffer from many of the disabilities that my doctors thought I might suffer from because of the injury to my left frontal lobe. My memory has been permanently damaged. I went from almost being able to remember my first steps, my address and phone number when we lived in Arizona, to not being able to remember events that occur in my everyday life. To be sure, I have learned to compensate for my memory loss and other disabilities and have developed other parts of my brain that were not accessible before the lightning. I live with my new disabilities and understand that God has given me other talents. I guess my being alive was enough for my parents because both of them had given up on raising me years before.

Life after Lightning

Later that summer, my dad took my older brothers Rich and Clarence with him to Kentucky. He showed them the land that he owned, and told them they would inherit it after his death. They met our relatives and learned more about his side of the family. Me, he left home and I pretty much took care of myself. While they were gone, Debbie and I moved her into her own apartment. We were worried about my graduating, leaving home and her living alone with my dad. We didn't want to take the chance of my dad using his power to abuse her either emotionally or sexually. Debbie was smart, independent minded, and was ready to make it on her own.

When my dad returned from Kentucky, he found me in our apartment, smoking weed. As he stood in the doorway, I could see that he was shocked that I moved all the furniture close to the walls, and had cleared the middle of the room. I knew that he was going to be angry that I moved Debbie out, and I wanted to give myself the advantage of having no furniture to obstruct my use tae-kwon-do, or nun-chucks.

As he stood in the doorway, I sprung from my seat, performed two high flying tae-kwon-do kicks, spun around and grabbed my nun-chucks that were hanging on the wall where his favorite picture used to be hung, and I began to swing them. I swung those nun-chucks for 15 minute, and was dripping with sweat, before he left without entering our apartment. My dad was a big man and could have attacked me. In fact, I invited his attack, but he didn't take the bait. I wasn't afraid of death, and I was convinced that one of us may not have survived his attack. He never said anything to me about that day, ever.

The next day, he came home only to find that Debbie had moved out of the apartment. He was angry and said, "Boy, you'ed betta move Debbie back home." I had stood up to my dad many times as a child, and he whipped me. This time was different, I was armed with nun-chucks that I wore around my neck, and he knew that I knew how to use them.

I told him, "not a chance" to his face. I was not a scared child anymore. I stood my ground, looked him in the eye, put my hands on my nun-chucks and invited him to attack. He didn't. The threat of violence left his eyes, and I saw a man who had relied on his superior strength to inflict pain on weaker people come to the realization that that his days of intimidating me were over. He walked passed me, went to his room and slammed the door shut, no discussion.

About a week later, my brother Joe came home from Boulder and said, "Man, dad's gonna kill you if you don't move Debbie back home." I couldn't believe my dad called him. As the dutiful son of a solider that he was, he delivered our dad's message. We had gone through this before in Chicago, when I was a 12 year-old child. Joe intimidated me back then, now I was bigger than he was, stronger too, and I laughed at the thought of him delivering my dad's threat. After all these years, he still saw himself as my dad's enforcer. I got this wild and crazy look in my eyes and said, "Forget about it." I lived with my dad, I thought to myself, why didn't my dad deliver the threat himself? That thought brought a smile to my face.

Joe looked at the strength in my arms, saw muscle with bulging veins, and said, "If I cut your arm, you would bleed all over the place." His comment was not a threat, but an acknowledgement that I had grown into a young adult and was powerful enough to defend myself from a physical attack. I said, "Do it." The smile never left my face. I wasn't Rich. If Joe would have made any aggressive move towards me, I was prepared to bust him up. He didn't either. Joe left our apartment, and went looking for Debbie's apartment, and found it.

Two hours after Joe left looking for Debbie, Clarence came back to the apartment and told me that Joe found Debbie's apartment and that he was there. He said, "Joe told me to move Debbie back home, and when I said no, he attacked me." He said that they wrestled around for a few minute, but he was stronger than Joe. Clarence said, "I was pinning him to the ground when he stuck his finger in my eye and tried to poke my eye out." Clarence told me, that when he complained to Joe about trying to poke his eye out, Joe said, "there aint no rules to fighting." When Clarence released him, he said Joe ran to the kitchen and got a steak knife and tried to stab him. I guess Joe thought he could get away with stabbing Clarence. Clarence said, "I ran to my car and grabbed that steel pipe that I carry around, and was headed back up to Debbie's apartment to beat Joe's brains out, when Bernard stopped me and told me not to hit Joe with the pipe. So I came over here to get you."

I grabbed my nun-chucks, and we went back to Debbie's. Joe was gone. Debbie put him out soon after Clarence left. Clarence and I searched the city for Joe, but he was nowhere to be found. I don't think he wanted to be found. Had Clarence and I found him, we were going to show Joe what "no rules" fighting really meant. Debbie never moved back home, and my dad never said a word to me about it, neither did Joe.

IN THE BELLY OF THE BEAST

After graduating third from the bottom of my high school class, I tried to join the United States Marine Corps. I went down to the recruiting station and signed the papers. They put me on a bus to Denver for testing. I spent the night in Denver, partied with other recruits on what I thought was my last night of freedom, and went in for testing the next day.

After a full day of testing, the recruiter told me that I passed all the tests except for the hearing test, and that they could not take me. I demanded to retake the test, and they agreed. I went back into the testing booth, put on the head set, and waited for the beeps. By now, I understood that the beeps got lower and lower until I could not hear them anymore. To improve my score, I clicked the clicker two more times, perfectly timed, in sequence, after I couldn't hear the beeps anymore. The tester acknowledged that my scores improved, but he was concerned because I pressed the clicker two more times after the test was over. My deception was uncovered and the Marines rejected me from serving my country.

When they put me on the bus for home, I realized that as a Marine, I was going to hurt people, maybe even kill some, and the anointing on my life was to help. I tried to convince myself that, as a Marine, I was actually going to help people. To be sure, I was signing up because I was hoping to serve my country in combat, and my personal goals went against my anointing. I cried on the bus trip home and apologized to God for not being obedient. I knew God had plans for me, the problem was, I didn't know what they were so I went back home and enrolled in Pikes Peak Community College (PPCC).

I attended PPCC for a year and a half and did the best I could. My problem was that I still couldn't read and write very well, and now I couldn't hear very well. After flunking out of PPCC, it was time for me to make it on my own. When I turned nineteen, and had recovered, at least physically, from being struck by lightning, I needed my own place. I paid $500 and bought a 1967 Plymouth Fury III. It had a lemon yellow color body with a black top. I called it The Lemon. A soldier sold it to me. It had a 383 cubic inch motor under the hood, was supped-up, and had decent tires.

I found a job as a janitor working for Garden of the God's Camp Grounds. I kept the grounds and restrooms clean during the early morning hours, and sometimes took on additional work as a day laborer for the owners' construction company. The problem with moving out was my timing. I hated living with my dad, and hated even more that I needed him to provide shelter a little while longer. I couldn't stand living with him any longer. I prayed, packed my belongings into the trunk of my car, and left home.

I went to work early in the morning, worked all day, and went to my construction job later in the day. I was tired and hungry but I had to save every dime I made so that I could afford to put a security deposit down on an apartment, pay the first month's rent, and buy gas to get back and forth to work. I slept in my car for a week, showered at the campgrounds, and ate at Howard's Pit Bar-b-q restaurant, free. My friend Reggie's dad owned the restaurant and his dad later hired me to work for him.

It was a hard week. Sometimes the police shined their flashlights into my parked car, woke me up, and told me that I couldn't sleep where I was parked and had to move on. The problem was I had to conserve my gas so that I could make it back and forth to work. It was cold at night and sometimes I needed to run my car for heat. I was dead tired, short on gas and hungry. I prayed. I needed more gas to keep warm at night, and had to save every dime I had for my deposit. I drove back to my dad's house, cut his garden hose, removed the gas cap from his car and siphoned gas from his car into mine. Taking some of my dad's gas was the only solution I could think of at the time, and it worked.

When I got paid, I rented a small apartment across the street from Prospect Lake. That first night in my own place was heaven. I felt no pain, had no TV, no radio, no food, but it was mine. I stretched out on the bed with no sheets and slept like a log. When I went to work the next day, I was a new man. The smile never left my face as I emptied the trash-cans, washed the toilets, and was nice to the customers.

I didn't have to go to work early to shower. I washed my clothes at the Laundromat, and provided for myself. If this wasn't heaven, I could sure see it from there.

After several months of being on my own, living on a shoestring budget, I stopped by the Four Seasons Hotel for a beer on my way home from work. I had grown to 6 feet 2 inches tall and looked rugged, dirty for sure. The bar tender was used to serving men that looked like me because the Springs is a military town, and I could easily have been a soldier. That beer tasted soooo good, Miller truly was the High Life.

As I finished my beer, and readied to leave the bar, an older woman, probably 30-35 stopped me and said, "Did your mother let you out tonight?" She was white, attractive, about five feet six inches tall and had nice figure. A little surprised that she spoke to me, I stopped, smiled, looked her in the eyes and said, "Sure, and she said I can do whatever I want to tonight." The lady smiled and ordered another Miller for me and a chardonnay for herself. We sat at the bar, enjoyed our drinks, and each other's company.

Brenda was from Ohio and was in town for a conference. On this trip, her entourage had gone to Denver on a scheduled outing and she stayed behind at the hotel. Her colleagues called earlier that evening to let her know that Monument, a small highway town nestled in the hills between Denver and Colorado Springs, was closed and that they had to spend the night in Denver. After telling me the story about her companions, she said, "I don't want to eat alone. Do you wanna join me for dinner?" I said, "Bet." I had been eating Howard's bar-b-q for weeks, so I wasn't about to turn down a meal at a hotel restaurant.

As we left the bar to go to the hotel restaurant, we learned that the restaurant seating area was about to close, and she said, "Do you mind if we order room service?" I said, "Not at all." We walked through the hotel, took the elevator to the third floor, and went to her room, which was actually a suite. She said, "Why don't you order while I slip into something more comfortable. I'll have steak, medium rare." I smiled at the thought, picked up the phone, and ordered a couple of steaks, one cooked to medium and the other to medium rare. I also asked them to send up a bottle of the red wine, right away. They delivered the wine and I had a glass, while I waited for Brenda to change.

I thought she was going to change into some blue jeans and a sweatshirt. After all, my blue jeans were dirty and I had on a lime green work shirt that my job provided, and steel-toed work boots. Why is it that company's make their employees dress up like clowns? Brenda did change into something more comfortable, a white, fishnet, Cleveland Browns jersey with only panties underneath. She also let down her long dirty-blond hair that she had pulled back, and tied neatly into a bun, on the back of her head. She was striking, but I pretended not to notice. I poured her a drink and we talked about football. She may have been from Ohio, but she was in Denver Bronco country. The busboy brought up the steaks; we ate and finished the wine. We talked until late into the night. She invited me to spend the night. I did.

In the morning, I showered, kissed Brenda one last time, went home, changed clothes, and went to the Lake. That is what we called Prospect Lake, which is at Memorial Park. In the Springs, in the 1970s, people went to the Lake for picnics and recreation, some to fish, others to play outdoor basketball. Some people went there to sell and buy illegal drugs or sexual favors. The Lake was the place to see and be seen, cruise your ride, and generally hang out. At the Lake, women of the night, became ladies of the day and showed off their prized assets.

I knew lots of people at the Lake and got caught up on the goings on in the city. My friends sat around, gambled, smoked weed, and we made plans for the night. It was Saturday, and the Springs was a sleepy city with few choices for nightlife. My friends Terry, Carl and I agreed to go to Denver later that night. We all had a little change in our pockets and I agreed to drive if they chipped in for gas. They agreed and our plan was set.

I picked Carl and Terry up at Terry's mom's house, got gas, and headed up I-25 towards Denver. We were all big men, Terry was all of 6 feet 3, I had grown 6 feet 2, and Carl was 6 feet even. We talked about the ladies we were going to pull, and the fun we were going to have, when Carl started talking trash. We all talked trash, and joined in the fun until he got tired of my talking about his big, booty-lips, and nappy head and said, "You'ed betta ease up off a brotha befo I whup yo ass." Terry was one of my best friends and was riding shotgun. Carl was in the back seat. I squinted my eyes and wrinkled my forehead as I adjusted my rearview mirror so I could see him and said, "You gonna whip whose ass?" Carl said, "Yo ass nigga." I pulled the car over and Carl and I got out. Terry tried to play peacemaker but I wasn't having any of it. If Carl wanted a piece of me, he was going to get it. He squared up on me, and I dropped him with a lightning quick right to his jaw. That was it, one punch and the fight was over. Terry went over and helped Carl get up. I said, "You wanna whip some mo ass nigga?" Carl shook his head no. We got back in the car and drove to Denver.

Later on that evening, we hooked up with my brother Rich, who was pimping and dealing drugs at the time. Rich always had a way with the ladies and we were pleased to go wherever he said the action was. We went to the 19th Hole and ended the night at Pierre's Supper Club. We all had a good time, but the news of the night was that Rich had bought a small, two-bedroom house, on Five Points. He bought the house as an investment and wasn't living it. He said that I could live in the house, if I wanted to move to Denver. All I had to do was pay the utilities, and take care of the place. I agreed to do it and within a month, I quit my job and moved to Denver.

LIFE ON THE FIVE POINTS

When I got to Denver, I learned that Rich hung out with a rough crowd. Cle, Duck, Ricky and Delano were about as dangerous a group of men as you wanted to come across in Denver. Rich and his friends ran a good portion of the night activities going on in Denver. I was the new kid on the block, and I was family. Nonetheless, I had to earn their respect.

I liked Cle and Ricky and didn't mind hanging around with them. What I didn't like, was that Ricky stopped by the house and let himself in. He told me that he didn't have to knock, because his sister owned half of the house. I couldn't argue with him about that, but I was living in the house and said, "Look bruh, jus knock." Ricky was straight-up gangster, and said, "Whatcha gonna do if I don't?" Ricky was quick, known to carry a straight edge razor, and had a well deserved reputation. His question was a threat, and not one to be taken lightly. What Ricky didn't know, was that I wasn't one to talk trash about what I was going to do. I attacked and took him down. We broke most of the furniture in the living room, and scuffed up the hardwood floor pretty good. In the end, Ricky agreed to knock before I released him from the chokehold that I put on him.

In the Springs, the scuffle would have ended our disagreement, in Denver, it didn't. Ricky came back to the house with his older brother Cle, and Cle was armed. He walked in, without knocking, took a pistol from this belt and fired it into the ceiling. I was unarmed, yet unafraid, because I didn't fear death. When my life flashed before my eyes, I saw the future, but I only remembered it as Déjà vu moments. This was one of those moments. I experienced that eerie feeling that this scene played out, and that my life would continue. I offered them a drink of Seagrams VO Canadian whisky; they accepted, and Cle offered me a cigarette. I took the pack.

Cle always had fascinating stories to tell and he entertained us for an hour or so. When they left, I changed the lock on the front door and hit the road back to the Springs. I wasn't running, I went to the Flee Market and bought a brand new, blue steel, cherry wood handle, Smith and Wesson nine millimeter, semiautomatic pistol and two clips. I stopped by another table and picked up a couple of boxes of shells and a shoulder holster. I hit the road and was back in Denver within a few hours. The next time Ricky and Cle showed their face in my house, I planned to enforce my own brand of justice.

My problems all changed when Rich separated from his wife and moved in with me. Now Rich had someone he could trust with his life and I had someone who could watch my back as well. If you messed with either of us, you had to deal with both of us.

It wasn't long before I got rid of my 67 Plymouth and bought a Gold, 1969 deuce-and-a-quarter. I was ready to roll, armed and dangerous, just like the players in Chicago.

I had been eating neck-bones, and beans and rice that Rich showed me how to make, for several weeks and I needed a job. Rich needed someone to collect his debts, and offered me the job. I accepted and patrolled brick city, that's what we called the projects, just behind our house on Five Points. Rich paid cash, and I set my own hours.

After a few weeks, I bought a gold pocket watch and chain, llama skin boots with gold trim spurs on the heels, virgin wool Italian suits to wear, and Cognac to drink. Ricky and Cle liked Hennessy. I preferred Courvoisier. I smoked a little weed every now and then and experimented with cocaine, but never became a user. In this line of work, it was better to keep a clear head because you never could predict what a drug addict might do.

One evening, Rich and I went to the lounge down the street from our house to hustle a few bucks playing pool. Rich was a shark and I was the set up man. I beat several local players while the marks, who thought they were sharks, watched. The stakes started as low as a dollar a game. After I beat the dollar players, the wannabe sharks raised the stakes to five dollars a game. I beat most of them until I got to the players who owned their own pool sticks and wanted to play for $10 a ball left on the table. The way it worked was, after the break, the looser had to pay $10 for each ball they had left on the table after the winner sank the 8 ball. By then, I had a few dollars in my pocket and the players were dangerous.

I usually played one or two $25 bucks a ball games, before getting beat and dropping $50 or $75 bucks on the table. That night, I lost and was looking for Rich to let him know it was time for him to play for high stakes, when I got intercepted by a fine sista who wanted to dance with me. When I was dancing, a brotha I owed money to stopped me on the dance floor and wanted his money. I reached into my pocked and came up short. Before I knew it, he hit me in the back of my head with a beer bottle. I was dazed, but not knocked-out, and I swung on him, just missing his head with a back-knuckle. When he dodged my blow, I attacked him driving him into a table where people were sitting. He was about to pull his pistol and shoot me when Rich showed up swinging. The back of my head was bleeding onto my white jacket and I stumbled outside as the bar cleared. I saw the brotha running down the alley and Rich narrowly miss hitting him with his car. I escaped death that night.

The next morning, the brotha showed up at our house to apologize to me. He didn't know that I was Rich's brother, and the word on the street was that Rich was going to set his Caddy on fire, with him in it. I accepted his apology. I saw that brotha one more time after that, at another bar. He was drunk, had his head down on the table, only to look up and see me standing there. By then, everyone knew that I packed a nine. He managed to get to his feet and he stumbled out of the bar. The word on the street was that the brotha left Denver, anyway, I never saw him again.

Life in Denver was hard. I tried to get a real job, but the amount of money I could make with a high school diploma, working a real job, made me feel like a chump. I did get a job, but when I walked down Welton Street to work or to workout at the 20th street gym, I had to walk right past a motor cycle gang's house. One day, the bikers were having a party and stopped me. They wanted to charge me to walk past their house. I wasn't about to pay, my cousin Craig taught me that lesson at age 12 in Chicago, so I made a deal with them. The deal was, I lived at the other end of their block, and that if I had to pay to walk past their house, they had to pay to ride their motorcycles past my house on the corner. They got a kick out of my offer, and let me pass without paying. When they rode their Harley's by my house and saw me out front strapped with a nine. They showed me respect and treated me like a brotha.

One evening, they invited me inside to see a part of their initiation process for membership in the gang. Their invitation was considered an honor for an outsider. They invited me in because I had earned their respect and had gained a reputation for being an enforcer for gangsters. Inside the house, they had a jukebox in the front room and Isaac Hayes' Shaft was blaring from the speakers. The men stood around, drinking, smoking, chewing tobacco and talking about the three B's; Booz, Bitches, and their Bikes.

The gang was originally from Chicago. They were surprised to learn that I had spent time in the Windy City too and they recognized the clubs and neighborhoods that I talked about. Soon, one of them offered me a smoke and I accepted. I had to wait for one of them to offer it to me, because to ask for a smoke would have meant that I was trying to punk the dude I asked, and I knew better than that. These men were dangerous and they were responsible for bringing drugs into the city.

After a while, a biker drove his bike into the middle of room. It was a nice bike, a Harley. He let the kick stand down and got off. He looked as rough as any member in the gang. He stood about 6 foot, 4 inches tall, had a barrel chest, and smelt like he just rode his bike through a sewer. I stood to the side as the leader of the gang held an empty Folgers coffee can high in the air. Each member took turns putting something foul into the can and took a part off of the bike until there was nothing left.

They handed the can to the biker and he drank it. The big man put the can to his lips and all sorts of crap flowed from around his mouth, dropping to the ground as he chewed to get the mixture to go down. My stomach couldn't take it. I ran for the door, vomiting as I went. When I got to the front yard, I emptied my stomach of the rest of the food I had eaten earlier in the day. The men laughed and patted me on the back. They knew that I couldn't stomach being one of them, but they also knew that I had lived in Chicago and hadn't seen a thing. I walked home. My girl called that night; I wasn't feeling it and didn't want to see her. She came over anyway, brought dinner, fixed me a drink and spent the night.

The next morning, I took the day off. My girl fixed breakfast and we planned to spend the day together. After we ate, eggs, bacon, grits, and drank some coffee, we hopped in my Deuce and went to City Park. They had paddle-boats and I rented one. We paddled to the little island at the center of the lake, did a little coke and smoked some weed. We talked about our dreams, and how it would be better if I could make some legitimate money. I was at a crossroads. I had money in my pockets, for sure, and I set my own hours. As long as I did my job, no one said boo to me. But what about my future? I didn't have one, and deep down, I wasn't helping anybody.

As we drove back to my girls crib, I was thinking about how I could make an ordinary living. The problem was, my marketable skills were washing dishes and working as a janitor. I explored the drug world, but it was on lock down. I would have had to kill one of the major players to take over his territory, and then fight off his lieutenants as well. I would have had to fight the battle royal, all without going to jail. I didn't think I could go to prison for ten to twenty years and still make something of myself. Deep down in my heart, I really wasn't a thug. I was a young man who was trying to find his way on the mean streets of Denver. What I really wanted was to go to college. Football was out, but I wasn't helping too many people and God spared my life again.

A few weeks went by and my LEAP check came to help me pay the utilities. I drove up the street to the corner store to cash the check. When we got inside, Rich wanted the money because it was his house. He made some risky investments, and one of his "friends" made off with the loot. I had been paying the utilities according to our agreement, but Rich demanded that I give him the money, right out in public. I don't know what he thought he was doing, but what I did know was that he wasn't about to punk me in public, in private or anywhere for that matter. When I refused, he kicked me in the family jewels, snatched the money, and had the nerve to go outside and get in my car. I got in the driver's side and told him that he owed me an apology. He told me that he didn't owe me shit. I said, "Get the hell out." Rich shot back, "I aint gettin outta shit." When I began to open my car door with my left hand, and reached down to turn the ignition off with my right, he sucker punched me in the eye. It was a hard shot and blood splattered on my car seat. When I saw the blood, I attacked him. He climbed over the seat and got out of the car through the back door. I drove off, back door still open.

When I looked at my eye in the rear-view-mirror, it was bleeding, and had begun to close. I drove to the clinic and the doctor saw me immediately. It took four stitches to get the bleeding to stop. The doctor bandaged my eye and told me to put a steak on it to keep the swelling down. I bought a steak, drove home, and did just that. I also took a couple of aspirin and washed them down with a shot of cognac.

I was sitting home fuming, with a steak on my eye, when Rich walked in. He was in no mood for talking and neither was I. I stood up and demanded an apology. My mom had taught me that first you asked for respect, and if that doesn't work, than demand it. If that doesn't work, take it, but don't leave without it. Just when he was about to tell me that he didn't owe me shit again, I reached back to my ancestors in Egypt, and delivered a right cross to his jaw. I was sure that I hit him hard enough to knock him out. I had it all planned out. While he was out, I was going to rummage through his pants pockets and take the money. It didn't happen. He took two or three steps back, but didn't fall.

Rich had a huge neck, and I remember my dad telling me that it was hard to knock-out someone if they had a big neck. I could see the rage building in his eyes, and I attacked him, driving him to the ground using my shoulder as a weapon. We wrestled around on the floor for a few minutes, and delivered some hard punches, before we both realized what we were doing. When we stopped fighting, Rich had a fat lip and couldn't get his mouth to stop bleeding. He gave me a dirty look, and went to the same clinic that I had gone to just moments ago. He saw the same doctor, and it took four stitches to get the bleeding to stop. The doctor told him to go home and put a cold steak on it to keep the swelling down.

When Rich came home, he had a fat lip, stitches, and a steak on his mouth. I laughed at the sight of him, and he laughed the site of me with a steak on my swollen eye. We agreed not to fight again. He did apologize for kicking me in the balls, but not for taking the LEAP check. I needed a new direction. Life on the Five Points was not for me. At one point in my life, I was mean enough to make it. Things changed after I got struck by lightning and I knew that God wanted me to help people and not hurt them. I was at the crossroads.

Part V

Temptation and God's Way

CHAPTER 8

EMILY GRIFFITH OPPORTUNITY SCHOOL AND ADULT EDUCATION

Nineteen eighty-two, I was twenty-two years old and my mom had moved to Aurora, Colorado, a Denver suburb. Clarence was living with her. A year earlier, Clarence was living with my dad in the Springs, his doctor diagnosed him with a chemical imbalance and put him on medication. Before he stabilized on his meds, my dad kicked him out of the house, no job, no money, no car, nothing. Clarence moved out and slept in abandoned houses in the neighborhood. It was all he could do to survive.

I saw Clarence on the street and he looked bad. His beard was overgrown, scraggly looking, and he was hearing voices. It took all of his energy to suppress the irrational voices in his head. I was furious. I drove to my dad's house, went in and confronted him. I was unarmed at the time, but not afraid. I would have fought him man to man. My day wasn't about to risk taking an ass whipping, especially from his son. He pulled a knife and tried to stab me. I was quick enough to get out the way of his lunge, and I managed to make it outside to my car. I opened the car door and stood my ground. I knew that I had a twelve inch stick on my car seat that I had treated with special oil until it was almost as hard as petrified wood. I expected him to advance on me with his knife. I planned to beat him about the head and body. I remembered all of those times he beat me mercilessly, and I planned to return the violence. My dad didn't know what kind of weapon I had, but he knew that I might have nun-chucks inside, and that I knew how to use them. He stopped his pursuit of me at his front door. I invited him to bring it, and called him a bunch of nasty names. He refused to take the bait. He stood his ground, at least for a moment, until I grabbed my stick and headed for the porch. He retreated into the house and locked the door behind him.

Clarence moved to Aurora to live with my mom and I stopped by to visit and to talk to her about my plans to go college and earning a degree. She always encouraged me to go back to school, but I had the usual excuses, no money, living expenses, yadda, yadda, yadda. None of my excuses held water. The truth of the matter is that I was afraid to fail. All of my brothers and sisters had tried college, none of them graduated, and they were all smarter than me. I had already flunked out of community college and there was no reason for me to believe that I could succeed in college where my brothers and sisters failed. I prayed.

The next week, I enrolled at Emily Griffith Opportunity School. That little voice in the back of my head reminded me that I had always been pretty good at math, so I enrolled in the Accounting Clerk Certificate program. My teacher was a sister, a little nerdy, but not bad looking. It took me nine-months to complete the program, all the while; I worked odd jobs to sustain myself. I was a busboy at a hotel, a cook at a restaurant, anything to keep me going and off the streets of Denver.

I met Dee at Emily Griffith. Dee was a fine sista, about 5ft. 6 inches tall, Caramel complexion, with a Coke bottle body and street smarts. At first glance, neither of us could hide our physical attraction to each other. We talked for a short time and sat side-by-side in class. I should have been listening to my instructor and thinking about my accounting lessons, but Dee was fine and my mind kept drifting back to how good she looked. During breaks, we got to know each other better and found that we had a lot in common. For lunch, we walked down Welton Street to my house and made out before going back to school. We decided that the trip to my house took too long, and we were missing too much school, so we often found empty classrooms and made-out at school.

I liked Dee. She was more like a partner in crime than a girl friend, but when we got the urge or needed to kill time, we shared the passion of each other's company. The funny thing about Dee was that my mom liked her. Little did she know, Dee and I spent more time discussing crime than we did discussing schoolwork. Whenever Dee came with me to visit my mom, we showed each other so much genuine affection that we looked like a couple. Dee fixed my food and brought it to me, and I thanked her with a kiss on her full, tender lips. That always made my mom smile. In our house, growing up in the 1960s, I had five sisters and a mom and my sisters did most of the cooking and cleaning. It made my mom proud that Dee happily served up my food and made sure that I had everything I needed. Dee wanted to please me, and she did, often.

After Dee and I graduated from Emily Griffith with Accounting Clerk Certificates, I took a job at Bennigans as a fry cook, so I had change in my pockets. I was looking for a way to get back into college, when I received a call from my mom. She needed my help. She told me that my brother Clarence went off his meds and was running down the street naked. I drove to my moms, parked, and her husband Andy and I went out looking for him. Luckily, we found him, sure enough, running down the middle of the street buck-naked. I jumped out of the car, caught him, covered him with my overcoat, and we brought him back home. Mom and I drove him to the hospital where he checked himself in for psychiatric treatment.

That evening, I told mom of my desire to go back to school. She always encouraged me and said that I could stay with her while I went back to school. It wasn't long before Andy passed away and she asked me if I would help her with my brother. She moved into a larger apartment and I put my few belongings in the trunk of my Deuce and moved in with her and my brother. The next day, I enrolled at CU Denver and took four courses. I later dropped one, but I completed the other three with more than a 2.0 GPA. I didn't know it at the time, but my GPA was important. I had flunked out of community college, and to transfer to another college, I needed to have made satisfactory academic progress at another university before I could be admitted to attend any out of state college. I also knew that I didn't want to attend CU because most of my older brothers and sisters attended CU and none of them graduated.

In the Fall of 1983, my mom and I drove my sister Debbie to Tempe Arizona to attend law school at Arizona State University. Debbie was the first person in our family to earn a Baccalaureate degree, and she did it at one of the most prestigious colleges in the state. It was a pleasant drive, and the campus was beautiful. The funny thing was that I had planned to attend ASU before I got struck by lightning, and seeing the campus made me realize that this is where I wanted to be. My athletic talents would have gotten me in school, but I would have had to pass college level courses to stay in school for four years. My success at Emily Griffith, and CU Denver, gave me the confidence I needed to believe that I could be successful at ASU.

As my sister settled into her dorm, I made my way across campus to the admissions office. They gave me the paperwork and admissions criteria. The admissions counselor told me that I could apply as a transfer student and apply my credits from CU Denver towards my degree at ASU. I completed the paperwork and applied for admissions for the Spring semester, 1984.

In the winter, 1983, I wrecked my Deuce going to my new job at UPS. The streets were icy, my ride was big, and my tires were bald. I worked as a truck unloader, and moved from there to a truck loader. I made decent money for working part-time, and the work was hard. I didn't mind the hard work, and this was Christmas season, so there was plenty of overtime.

Dee and I were seeing less and less of each other. She maintained her street-life ways, and I was moving in another direction. Our relationship officially ended when she got pregnant. Dee later told me that she wanted to have a baby, and had to choose between me and anotha brotha. She chose the otha brotha because he was a pimp, and she thought he had more streets smarts than I did. She may have been right.

Dee had her baby, but the baby had problems. Things got worse for Dee when her baby got a hold of some household cleaner, drank it, and had to be hospitalized. I am not sure what happened to the baby, but Dee was later hospitalized in a psychiatric ward of the local hospital. I went to see her, and she was happy to see me. She said that she regretted not having my kid, but what was done, was done. She asked me to visit her again, and this time to bring her a joint. I did and she smoked it on the ward. That was the last time I saw Dee.

THE FASHION SHOW

Life was changing for me. The more I walked away from my street-life ways, the more blessings I received. Earlier in the spring, my sister-in-law invited me to a fashion show. I accepted and we sat at a table sponsored by her job. I met her and her friends at the show. While I may have been a cook and a UPS worker, I was still 6ft 2 inches tall, had nice clothes, and I wore a grey, pinned stripped, three piece suit to the show. As my mom used to say, I was clean as a chitlin.

We were seated at a table on the right corner of the stage. Models walked by, and had to turn at the corner of the stage, right at our table, to exit the stage. Several of the women smiled at me and otherwise signaled their approval. As the show went on, one of my street friends, who was working with the promoter, invited me back stage. We went back stage where the models frantically changed clothes, some changing hair, as they hurried back out to the ramp. He pointed out one young woman, and assured me that she was fine, fine, fine. I hadn't noticed her because she was not one of the models who smiled at me during the show. Nonetheless, there was a dance following the show and we socialized with the models. Local pimps took the opportunity to get wannabe fashion models hooked on drugs so they could turn'em out as common street hoes.

During the dance, I got several phone numbers and promised to make calls later during the week. After dancing with the model who my friend had pointed out, she asked for my number. I smiled at the thought of her request and gave it to her. I was single and there was no reason for me not to talk to any of those women. They were all fine and I was planning a move to Arizona anyway. From my days in the streets, I learned that men don't chase women, we attracted them. I also had a policy of not calling women for a week or two after getting their phone numbers. I forgot that I gave my phone number to one of the models, Bonnie, and she called to invite me out dancing with her and her roommate the following weekend. I accepted. I drove to the club and parked my wrecked Deuce way in the back of the parking lot, so no one would see me getting out of it, and went inside.

As I walked in, Bonnie spotted me right away. She was fine, just like my friend said. She was 5ft 8, had cinnamon colored skin, long hair and a nice figure. We talked and had a good time that night. Through our conversation, I learned that Bonnie was college educated, had book smarts, but was naïve in the ways of the street. We had fun that night and I kissed her goodbye; and we went our separate ways. I left the club a little early because I didn't want anyone to see me getting into my wrecked Deuce. From that day on, Bonnie called me early and often, she wanted to see me. In her day job, she was a receptionist for a large corporation. At night, she worked for a modeling agency. She worked hard and was nice to me.

I dated other women too and my mom didn't like any of them. She especially hated that I dated Joan, a Chicana sista, who was as hot as Gloria Estefan. Joan was four or five years younger than me, but we always had a good time hanging out. She was playful, and beautiful and fun to be around.

Joan and I were seeing each other on a regular basis, but Bonnie had designs on my heart. She invited me over for dinner and a movie, I accepted. I drove to her house that she shared with two other women, one of which owned the property. I parked my beat-up Deuce down the street from her house so no one would see me getting out of it. Dinner was superb, the conversation was nice, and the movie her roommate had rented was X-rated.

It didn't take long before Bonnie and I had to excuse ourselves from the living room where we were watching the movie with her roommate and her date. We stayed up late talking well into the night. She invited me to spend the night, I did. When I woke up the next morning, I could smell eggs, bacon and grits, with orange juice, toast and coffee. Bonnie was trying to put the moves on a brotha, and I was headed to Arizona in two months. I wasn't committing to any long term relationships, and didn't bother to tell Bonnie about my plans to attend college in January 1984. Bonnie and I got together as often as we could, and I took her home to meet my mom. She couldn't believe that I lived with my mom, or how beat-up my car was. None of those things mattered, she was falling in love, and she was planning on keeping me. Little did she know, in a matter of weeks, I was moving to Arizona to attend ASU.

The following day, Bonnie stopped by my mom's apartment, unannounced, and found me and Joan wrestling around on the grass out front. Undeterred, Bonnie gave me that look that black women give brothas when they want to kill us, but know they love us, and went inside. Anyway, my mom was home and let her in. I kissed Joan goodbye and told her that I would call her later, I did. Like Dee, my mom liked Bonnie. In private, mom admitted that she thought Bonnie was a little too young for me and a little slow, but she liked her. The funny thing was that Bonnie was two years older than me and had a college degree. I think my mom noticed that Bonnie didn't have much street smarts, which Dee had plenty of, but she liked her anyway.

I broke the news to Bonnie that I was going to ASU, and she was hurt. I wasn't in it to hurt anybody, but I had to get my life back on track. I got rid of my Deuce and bought a 1973 Oldsmobile Tornado for $250. It was all white, with maroon colored interior, and it sat on three flat tires, no dents. It took me a week to get the car running and I bought a set of used tires to put on it. I tuned up the engine, changed all the belts, fluids, and charged up the AC.

In January 1984, I packed up my things and headed to ASU. My sister Debbie flew back to Denver to make the road trip with me. I kissed my mom goodbye and hit the road. We stopped in the Springs to pick up a few personal items that Debbie had left with our sister Pam. Pam couldn't believe that I was going to college in Arizona, no one could.

CHAPTER 9

ARIZONA STATE UNIVERSITY WITH BARRY BONDS AND FRIENDS

January 1984, it was 80 degrees outside as Debbie and I rolled into Tempe, AZ in my new ride, no problems. I checked into the residence hall to receive my room assignment before I unpacked my car. I was 23 years old and had matured into a young man.

I couldn't help but to notice the women checking me out, as I was checking them out. I was in college now, at a big, intimidating school, now all I had to do was make it. All of my older brothers and sisters quit before earning a degree and I had flunked out of community college before earning a few transferable credits at CU Denver. Only Debbie earned a college degree and now she was studying law at ASU.

College was exciting. Everywhere I looked, thousands of young people, and some not so young but eager students like me, all in one place determined to make better lives for ourselves, or at least have fun trying. I enrolled second semester, so many of the students already knew each other. I didn't know a sole, outside of my sister.

The residence hall director assigned me to a room with three roommates. When I opened the door, the smell was nauseating. Dirty clothes, smelly tennis shoes, dirty dishes, pizza boxes, beer cans, vomit, you name it and my dorm room had it on the floor waiting to greet me. I took one look, shut the door, and headed back to the residence hall director's office. The residence director understood, and assigned me to a new room with a single roommate. This room was clean and neat, and I accepted it.

Cholla Hall was more like apartments than dorm rooms. I had a room to myself, with a joining bathroom to my roommate's room, a kitchen, living area, and a balcony. There were four independent complexes with a common pool and volleyball court in the middle. We also had an onsite weight facility. I secured a student loan to pay my tuition, room and board, bought books and school supplies. Then I made my way to the pool. For three weeks straight, I walked by the pool and never made it campus. I was overwhelmed by the culture of my new surroundings at ASU, and it was difficult to focus on my studies. The women of Cholla were stunning as they sunned themselves by the pool every day, and wore as little as they could get away with, short of being naked. I didn't need a tan, but sitting on the edge of the pool, in January, and talking to near naked coeds was alluring.

Cholla had its own subculture rules. My floor had one rule, if you got invited to the party on the floor, you agreed not to report the party to the Residence Hall Assistant who lived on another floor. Every night, for the entire semester that I lived at Cholla, I got invited to parties in different rooms. The dorms were coed and four attractive coeds lived across the hall from me. They were friendly too and often cooked breakfast for me in the morning. In my mind, men used women for cooking, cleaning or pleasure, and some used them for making money.

I got to know the Cholla residents quite well; my problem was that I hadn't cracked a book nor made it to any of my classes for three weeks. One morning, I was headed to the pool when one of the young ladies who lived across the hall asked me if I was ready for our psychology exam. We all knew each other's class schedules, but I was shocked to learn about the exam. I didn't even know where my class was, so we went to class together. I took the exam and failed it. My failure brought back all sorts of bad memories from my past failures, but I wasn't about to give up, at least not yet.

The next day, I went to class and met some of my classmates. I also met some people who later became my friends. One of my new friends, Barry Bonds, also lived at Cholla. We became friends and hung out together.

When Barry and I met, he introduced himself to me as Barry Bonds and I introduced myself as David Caruth. Barry thought I said David Carew and asked if I was related to Rod Carew. I kidded him and said yes, that I was Rod Carew's nephew. Barry's eyes lit up. He told me that he loved Rod Carew and that Carew had the sweetest swing in baseball. This was high praise coming from Bobby Bonds' son and Willie Mays' Godson. Carew was one of his all time favorite players, and Barry thought I looked a little like him as well. I laughed at the thought. Most of the people on campus mistook me for Byron Scott, the shooting guard for the Los Angeles Lakers who starred at ASU. I was surprised that so many people took a liking to me, even after finding out that I couldn't ball like Byron, play baseball like Barry, and couldn't come anywhere near their athletic prowess.

On the outside, I had strong, lean, athletic looking body like Barry's, and I liked to keep in shape.

David Caruth, freshman year, Arizona State University, 1984.

Inside, I was wondering if I had what it took to succeed. As Barry and I jogged around campus, he tried to talk me into walking on the baseball team and even offered to introduce me to the coach. To keep the accidental joke going, I told Barry that I was thinking about it, and let him know that I was fast and could probably out run him. I was fast, and not short on confidence, but didn't know if I could really beat him in a race. He smiled that famous, Barry Bonds smile, and accepted my challenge, on the spot.

Since I challenged him, I told him to count, and that we would go on three. He agreed and started counting. When he hit three, we took off like greyhounds. I actually got the jump on him. Barry learned right away that I could go from zero to fast in a matter of seconds. For the first 20 to 30 yards, I was running ahead of him. But Barry was a great athlete, and a powerful runner. Just before he blew passed me, as my friend Tim had done in seventh grade, I shut it down and acted like I let him catch up. The truth of the matter was that I could feel him gaining ground on me with every step before I shut it down.

Barry was impressed with my speed, and invited me over to the athletic department so I could meet the coach. He was psyched about meeting

Rod Carew's nephew, and possibly playing ball with him at ASU. I was dying laughing inside and couldn't stand it any longer so I told Barry my real name. We both got a laugh out of it. I told him that I was really an ex-football player and that lighting ended my career in high school. Like most people, he couldn't believe my story, but I told it anyway. We stayed friends and made plans to go out that night.

When we went out, we took Barry's car because my car was a $250 hooptie, and Barry had a Trans Am. I remember his license plate read, BBSTA, which stood for Barry Bond's Sweet Trans Am. We shared stories about our lives, and it was an eye opening experience for me to hear Barry talk about growing up as Bobby Bonds' son. He talked about how his dad and Willie Mays endured prejudice and racial epithets in the major leagues and how reporters focused on any negative detail they could find to write something negative about black athletes.

Barry's firsthand account of the media helped him develop a stand-offish approach to interacting with the media and he carried that mistrust with him into his pro career. Barry's stories of his dad reminded me of the stories my dad told me about seeing more Confederate flags, than American flags, when he was at war in Korea. Because Barry was with his dad, it was easier for me to internalize Barry's dads experience with racial prejudice than it was my own dad's. Knowing my dad's faults, up close and personal, made me dismiss his experience with racial prejudice and I even thought he deserved some of the poor treatment he received.

When Barry and I went to the clubs surrounding ASU, we took our pick of the women whose company we wanted that night. There was no shortage of pretty women at ASU, and Barry and I walked out of the club or party with women who rated 10.5 on a 10-point scale. The white boys hated it, but Barry and I were both good size men with something extra. Barry was supremely confident because he had grown up knowing he was a special talent and everyone knew it. I, on the other hand, had a confidence that came from walking with dangerous men, and knowing that the white boys whose testosterone may get the better of them every once in a while, were still boys who had gone straight from high school to college, with little life experience in between. For whatever reason, the white boys never challenged Barry or me.

At the end of my first semester, Barry and I moved into the same apartment complex, across the street from Cholla, and continued our friendship. There were always things going on in Tempe and one evening,

OP Shorts sponsored a competition at Big Surf, an outdoor swimming park complete with beach sand and waves. One of the girls I met at Cholla had taken a picture of me wearing some shorts and sent it in, along with my phone number. I was surprised when I got a call and an invitation to compete in the live competition, with the winner walking away with a new motorcycle. Barry and I went. I was on stage, wearing OP Shorts and vying for applause, and Barry was in the crowd hooking up our dates for the evening. The winner came down between a white boy and me. I thought I received more applause, but the judges gave the bike to the white boy. No matter, Barry had pulled two 10.5's and we made plans to go out that night.

Barry and the two strikingly beautiful, blond-hair, blue-eyed, bomb shells were ready to go; but I had to change clothes and put on some shoes so I could make the dress code for where we were going. All I had on was a muscle shirt, skintight OP shorts, and flip-flops. We all went back to my apartment in Barry's TA, so that I could change. None of us expected Barry's girlfriend to be waiting for us in her car, parked outside of my apartment. We were caught, red handed.

While Barry and his girl talked, I went inside, took a quick shower, and changed. When I returned, Barry's girl was pissed. I got in the back seat and we drove off. I asked Barry if he was cool with this and he said, "Ya, don't worry about it." In my world, if a brotha said don't worry about a woman, the conversation was over. There were tons of women to choose from, so she just had to get over any disappointment if she wanted to roll with us.

We went out that evening, to an upscale club, and had a great time. Our dates were from wealthy families, as was Barry. I was the only one who had grown-up in poverty and knew more about the streets than I did about social grace. Our dates had no idea that I learned to charm women from pimps who seemed to know the female mind inside and out. This knowledge and my experiences put my conversation at another level. We talked and danced the night away.

When we left the club, we went back to their place. Barry's car had to get buzzed past the guard. Once inside their apartment, I don't know what Barry did, but my date and I wasted no time getting better acquainted.

Later that summer, I enrolled in summer school and Barry went to training camp in Kansas City. I soon learned why all of my friends thought I was crazy for going to summer school. What they didn't know was that

I was a former special Ed student, had graduated third from the bottom of my high school class, had flunked out of community college, and that I had earned a 1.5 GPA my first semester at ASU. Most of my classmates were smart and belonged at ASU. I desperately needed to improve my academic performance or I was going to be suspended. Besides not wanting to be suspended from school, I also wanted to establish residency because I was paying out of state tuition. I had to show that I had actually moved to Arizona by living in the state for a year. There was no question that I met the residency requirement of being an adult student, with no hope of parental support, so I braved the heat. I think that was the last summer I spent in Tempe. The next year, I got resident status and saved a couple thousand dollars in tuition.

My first day of summer school, I walked to campus, which was a few blocks away from my apartment. Boy was that ever a mistake! It was 120 degrees outside that day, and when I arrived at school, I had sunburn on the top of my head. I may not have been book smart, but I was smart enough to buy a hat for the walk home. I couldn't comb my hair for a week without pain.

After school, I went back to my apartment, put on my Speedo's, flip-flops, grabbed a beach towel and headed for the pool. I left my towel and flip-flops on the grass, in the shade of a Palm tree. The pool apron was so hot that I got blisters on my feet walking across it to the water. When I got out of the water, my feet were wet so I made it back to the grass without burning my feet again. I was a college student; going swimming wasn't supposed to be that tough. The next time I went in the water, I wore my flip-flops across the pool apron, jumped in, leaving them on side of the pool. Life was good.

That evening, I got a call from Barry. He was in Kansas City and he said, "Dave, man, I can't hit, can't run, and can't catch." I was shocked. Barry was the best baseball player in the country. I said, "What are you talking about man? Did you get hurt?" He said, "No, it's Les. She won't talk to me. Tell her to answer the phone." I said, "All right man. I'll tell her the next time I see her." I didn't that day. Around midnight, I got another call from Barry asking me if I had spoken to Les. I said "No" and he asked me to go over to her place and ask her to "please, please, please, answer the phone." I tried to protest, but either Les or I had to talk to Barry all night and I had other plans.

I walked over to her apartment and knocked on the door. She answered, through the door, "What?" I said, "Les its Dave, open up." She said, "No, it's Barry and I'm not talking to him." I pleaded with her, "Common Les, please, open the door, just for a minute." I don't know what it is about a man begging that gets women to do what we want, but it worked. Les opened the door and invited me in. I told her, "Les please, just talk to Barry for five minutes." I told her that it was my fault that she caught me and Barry the other night. I pleaded with her, "Just talk to him for five minute and I can go home." The whole time we spoke, the phone rang. She picked it up, and hung up, only for it to ring again in a matter of seconds. Finally, Les answered the phone. I showed myself to the door and went home.

The next day, Barry called to thank me and assured me that he was back. He had jacked a couple of homers, stole a few bases, and was throwing runners out at home plate from left field. I was happy for him, but it didn't end there. A few weeks later, Les stopped me on campus and said that she wanted to talk to me. I was busy doing my job cleaning off Kiosks on campus, so we set up a time to talk later that night. Les knew that Barry was my boy. The problem was that she was in love with Barry and was talking about marriage and having his babies. I was stunned. From what I could tell, none of us wanted to be married or have babies. I thought my friend was in trouble, or was about to be. All Les wanted from me was the truth. After all, she caught Barry and me with two women outside of my apartment, and even after we were caught, we went out and didn't make it back to our apartments until early in the morning.

I had never been in a position where I had to break a woman's heart, especially a woman who wasn't even my girl. I had never known love, just dating, and another date was always just around the corner. But this was different. Les meant something to Barry or he wouldn't have sent me over to her apartment a few weeks ago. But, love? Barry? We talked about women all the time, but we never talked about love. And Les wanted to have his babies?!

The rule on the street was that you never ratted on your friends, especially to women. I had a dilemma, go against man law and tell her the truth, or continue the lie that I told her earlier. I knew that I was supposed to help people, not hurt them. But did this count? At the end of the day, I decided that she was entitled to the truth. Besides, everyone we knew already knew that I was in the OP Shorts contest and that Barry had pulled the women. I rationalized, sooner or later, someone was going to tell her the truth. I told Les the truth and she broke it off with Barry. Somehow, telling the truth was liberating, at least for me anyway.

Later that Fall, I saw Barry and told him that I felt bad for telling Les the truth. Barry told me not to worry about it. In Denver, the men I hung with respected deception more than the truth, but at ASU, I earned Barry's respect by showing strength of character. We were still friends, Barry found another woman, and was happy. I don't know what happened to Les. For what it was worth, at least she didn't get pregnant and Barry didn't get trapped into a relationship that he didn't want for the sake of a kid, like so many other athletes do. Was I helping people? Who knows, but I think I did the right thing by telling Les the truth.

ARIZONA BLACK COLLEGIATE ATHLETES ASSOCIATION

The Fall semester was in full bloom, football season was underway, and we were supposed to have a good team. There were only about 400 Blacks on campus, so we pretty much all knew each other, partied together, or just hung out. That morning, I went to campus and learned that a young brotha from California was being charged with allegedly sexually assaulting a coed. His bail was set at $137,000. We were all stunned. Later on that evening, a group of us met at my apartment to talk about what happened. Several brothas I knew were at the party where the alleged rape took place. The accuser was known to have slept with several other football players, all of them black, and we were furious. It didn't have to be Vince who got accused; it could have been any of us. We had to do something, and fast. Just then, someone knocked on my door and it turned out to be the young woman who reported the crime. She was in tears, but we weren't feeling it. She begged us to listen. I invited her in.

She explained that she was from a wealthy family and that her dad found out that she was dating a black football player. He forced her to file the charges, or he was going to cut her out of his will, and take away her trust fund. We all knew that she was sleeping with Vince at the time, and that several of her friends would say that they left the party together. We also knew that any sex they had was consensual, so we had to do something. I prayed to God and asked him for courage and wisdom.

The next morning, I went down to the Student Life office and spoke with a friend of mine who was also on the football team. He hooked me up with the paperwork necessary to establish a student organization. I completed the application, turned it in, and the Arizona Black Collegiate Athletes Association was born. Now, all I needed was some members. I met with brotha after brotha and they all signed up. Somehow, almost overnight, I was transformed from the brotha from Denver, into a leader on campus. Perhaps the brothas on campus respected me for standing up and fighting for one of their own. I don't know for sure, but what I do know is that I risked angering powerful people, and my friends appreciated my courage. I sighed up football players, track stars, basketball players, and female athletes. Now, I needed to take action.

That evening, I called a meeting at my apartment and people showed up. We discussed how the black football players should walk off the field, at the start of the third quarter of our nationally televised game against UCLA. I agreed to negotiate with the television network to give me two minutes of airtime to explain why ASU's black players were walking off the field. A reporter for the Campus Weekly, one of two student run newspapers, got wind of our plan and asked to interview me. I gave her the scoop and she took a picture of Kim Hampton, Barry Bonds, and me for the front page. In the morning, the paper hit the newsstand and campus was buzzing. There was no time for classes that day, my friends and I had to organize a nationally televised strike beginning with our black football players for the upcoming weekend.

That evening, I received a call from ASU's President. He wanted to talk. Specifically, he wanted to know what it would take for me to call off the strike. I was both the organizer and President of the ABCAA, and for the time being, I had some clout. After all, ASU's best women's basketball player, its greatest baseball player, and I were on the front page of a student newspaper and we had over 40,000 students who were interested in why we were organizing.

It would have been nice had I known how to wield so much power, but as it was, I didn't, but I negotiated anyway. I told the President, "we want Vince out of jail immediately, and all the charges dropped." My request was modest, but the President still managed to put up some resistance. He explained that this was a criminal matter, and that there was nothing he could do to get Vince released from jail. Nevertheless, he promised to try. I told him that wasn't good enough, and soon, the entire nation was going see how black athletes were being treated at ASU, and I wasn't joking. I hung up the phone.

My friends who overheard the conversation thought I did well. I wasn't sure, until the next morning. The following day, Vince was a free man, and all the charges had been dropped. He had served 18 days in jail because his parents couldn't afford to post his bail. He was way behind in schoolwork and his position on the team was in jeopardy. Had I known better, I probably could have negotiated for his scholarship to continue and other concessions. I didn't, but Vince was free and he thanked us for it. Kim, Barry, me and other Black athletes stood side-by-side and held our ground.

Barry didn't have to support this cause, but those of us who got to know him, know that he is a man of character. He had the courage to stand for what he believed in, regardless of the consequences. If you want to talk about young people building character in college, this was it. This time, I really did help someone, no doubt about it. I didn't expect to go to ASU and become an activist like Stokley Carmicle and other student activist leaders that I heard about in the 1960s. I was pretty much a nobody but now, I noticed that white photographers were taking pictures of me as I walked across campus. In our society, there is always a cost to pay for having the courage to stand up to power in the face of injustice. My standing up for Vince at ASU put me on somebody's radar.

Soon, Barry got drafted by the Pittsburg Pirates. Before he rolled out of town, he stopped by my place and gave me Bobby Bond's home address and phone number. He told me that I could always reach him there. We shook hands, hugged, and agreed to keep in touch. As it turned out, Barry went on to become the greatest baseball player of our time. He also turned out be a dedicated husband and father as well. I know Barry Bonds, he's a friend of mine. When the final chapter his written on him, you will see that he was born to be the greatest baseball player of our time, and that he is a caring, God fearing family man who puts the needs of others above his own. I think we're similar in that respect.

I made other friends too, Smitty, Herman, Rob, and John to name a few of my closest friends. Herman, Rob, John and I all had a few years of life experience behind us. Smitty was three or four years younger than the rest of us, and I sort of adopted him. In the Spring semester of 1984, I would see Smitty rolling across campus in his power wheelchair, but we never stopped to talk to each other. Smitty had been at ASU for two years and pretty much hung around white boys who were interested in broadcasting.

That summer, when I was walking home from taking summer classes, I spotted Smitty on the other side of the street sitting idle on the sidewalk in his power wheelchair. It was blistering hot that day, and even I had learned to wear a baseball cap to keep the sun off my head. As I got closer, from across the street, I could see that he was not moving and traffic was passing him by as if he was a cactus in the desert. I dodged traffic and jaywalked across the street to find out what the problem was. It was way too hot outside for someone to be sitting in dessert heat for any extended amount of time.

When I approached Smitty, he was almost delirious. He was hot, dehydrated, and his wheelchair battery had died. He was stranded on the sidewalk, in 120-degree heat, and it looked like I was the only pedestrian to notice. I pushed Smitty's roasting-hot wheelchair back to my apartment, and offered him some lemonade. He couldn't thank me enough, and I tried to make him feel welcome. He said I saved his life that day, but I had to think that someone would have stopped and helped him had I not been passing by at just the right time. As he rested in my air-conditioned apartment, and re-hydrated with some cool lemon aid, I went to his place and got his battery charger. Smitty's battery was similar to a car battery, and his charger was similar to car battery charger as well. We talked while his battery charged and later became friends. When he got home, he called and thanked me again. He was welcome.

From that day on, whenever I saw Smitty on campus, he went out of his way to shake my hand and talk. As it turned out, Smitty really didn't have any black friends, and didn't even consider himself as black. He told me that he was disabled and that being black didn't have anything to do with his problems. I had enrolled in an African American Studies class with Dr. VP Franklin, and I begged to differ. I was a few years older than he was, and had experienced racial prejudice first hand as a child growing up and later on as an adult. Dr. Franklin was exposing me to more and more of the cruel realities that African Americans endured in the U.S. every day, and the ingenious ways our forefathers overcame them. Smitty may have been naive, and even a little ignorant about the struggles and accomplishment of his own race, but he loved to talk and quickly joined my circle of friends.

I don't think Smitty was enjoying ASU the way the rest of us were. That all changed when he started hanging out with me and my friends. We took Smitty partying with us, out to eat, and even swimming. He said that I tried to drown him in 4ft of water as I held him parallel to the water and walked him from one side of the pool to the other while he moved his arms as if he were swimming. He told me later that he wasn't swimming, but trying the best he could to keep his head from going under water. I was holding him up, but it was kind of funny to hear him tell it.

We carried his wheelchair up and down stairs to clubs and private parties. Don't get me wrong, Smitty wasn't shy, it was just that he didn't know how much fun the brothas at ASU were having. Smitty danced, had a few drinks, and even slow danced by way of a lap-dance in his chair when it was time pair up before the evening ended. His problem was that he didn't know how to close the deal, so we often had to drop him off at his apartment before we disappeared into the night with our female companions. That all changed when he met some of my other friends, most notably, Herman.

Smitty, left and Herm, right, outside of my apartment, Tempe, Arizona, 1986.

Herman and I met my first semester at ASU in Spanish class. We were the same age and were both pursuing degrees in Political Science. When I walked into class, a full three weeks after classes started, I saw a brotha sitting in the back of the class wearing sun glasses. Herm reminded me of one of my street friends from Denver, so I took a seat as far away from him as I could get, and next to a pretty, Spanish-looking girl. Herman looked as clueless as I was, and I thought he was probably going to flunk out college. After class, I was talking to Tina and arranging a study date for the evening. I was behind, and she was cute, bilingual, and just what the doctor ordered.

After class, Herman came up to me, held out his hand like brothas do and said, "Herm, wazz-up?" I took his hand, gave him the double handshake and said, "Dave, you got it bro." Herm was cool. It was almost as if he sensed that I was from the streets. I had planned for Tina and me to study together that night, but Herm managed to invite himself, and the three of us agreed to meet later that day to study Spanish.

As I got to know Herm, I found out that he had gone to Catholic school for a few years before attending a private elementary school for boys. He also came from a good family. His mom was a nurse and his dad had a Doctorate degree. The fact of the matter was, Herm was really pretty smart, and I was more likely to flunk out of school than he was. Herm's problem was that he didn't know what he wanted to do when he grew up. He was living in a run-down apartment, was attending classes at ASU, and worked as a bartender at a popular jazz club in Tempe. He invited me down to the bar that weekend, and I went. Usually, when I went to the bar, it was during happy hour so I could get something to eat. I usually had just enough money in my pocket to buy a cold beer. I took a seat at the bar. Herm, all 5 foot 7 of him, was busy mixing drinks and generally entertaining the other patrons who sat at the bar. It didn't take long for me to recognize a player when I saw one, and I spotted his little herd of groupies who were on the ready to do whatever he said in a moment's notice.

One evening at the jazz bar, I sat down to order a beer and Herm sat a double shot of Cognac down in front of me, no charge. It didn't take long for Herm to learn that I had grown accustomed to drinking good quality liquor from my days in the streets, and that the reason I was broke was because I was trying to change my ways. I appreciated his gesture and deposited my couple of dollars into his tip jar, and said, "Wazzup bruh?" My question wasn't small talk either. Herm knew what was going on in the bar and he knew, that I knew, that he knew. There really wasn't much going on that night so I checked out and went home early.

Later that evening, early in the morning, I got a call from Herm. He told me that he lent a girl his car, and that somehow, it got stolen. He asked me if I wanted to roll with him and Rob to look for his car. I grew up poor, lived on the Five-Points in Denver, and nothing about the streets of Phoenix intimidated me. I said, "Bet" got dressed, and they picked me up.

Our friend Rob was a Political Science major too. He was a cool brotha, about 6 feet tall, still wore a jerri curl, and was a few years older than both Herm and I. We headed straight to the hood, eyes peeled, and Herm was pissed. We visited several places where Herm thought we might find his car. We crashed parties, and cruised the red-light district without finding it.

I didn't know it at the time, but Herm had an established relationship with God too. We cruised around for hours, with little hope of finding his car. Herm prayed to God, right in front of Rob and me. His prayer was something like, "God, please let us find my car. If you do, I will give up all the stupid things I've been doing and change my ways." I almost couldn't believe it. When I prayed, God almost always took a week to answer my prayers. When Herm opened his eyes, his car turned directly into our path ahead of us. Rob hit the gas and the chase was on.

The thugs tried to lose us, but Herm's car was a Ford Escort that didn't have much power, even after they tried to accelerate. We stayed hot on their trail. Turn after turn, up streets, down alleys, we followed those criminals. Soon, Herman's car ran out of gas and the criminals jumped out of the car and made a run for it on foot. We should have secured Herm's car, but we didn't. We gave chase on foot and followed the criminals into a neighborhood house party. We were after those crooks and questioned the people at the party. We were in a dangerous part of town and somebody could have gotten hurt. Either the criminal we sought wasn't there or the party goers lied to protect him, but he got away. We drove back to Herm's car, gassed it up and went home.

The interesting thing about Herm recovering his stolen car that night was the promise he made to God to do what was right. He knew that he was involved with shady people, but he enjoyed the criminal element part of his life. After he made his commitment to change his ways, God gave me a partner who had to give up street-life, just like I was trying to do. Until that very moment, Herm's heart really wasn't into getting a college degree. Now, I had a friend who truly understood the sacrifice I was making to change my life, and someone who was as committed as I was to leaving a negative lifestyle behind. Early that morning, Rob dropped me by my apartment. We agreed to play hoops later in the day after we got some sleep. Herm was short, but he could play some ball. He was so good that we started calling him Spud Herm, after the pro player, Spud Webb.

My friend John was different from my other friends. Most notably, he was a 6ft. tall, blond haired, blue-eyed white boy from Mississippi, and a

Republican to boot. No matter, we all liked him and called him John the Republican.

Dave, left and John, right, Cholla Hall,
Arizona State University, 1984.

John and I met at Cholla and often crossed paths on the happy hour circuit, where we were more interested in the free food than the two for one drinks. Unlike my other friends, who were pursuing political science degrees, John was a finance major who had just completed a tour of duty in the US Air Force. Any day of the week, I could call John and ask him where we could eat free that day. John knew, and often swung by and picked me up. Sometimes I met him there. He drove a sporty, sky-blue, two-seat Mazda, so I understood that if he had a date, I had to make my own way home. Most of the places we went were in walking distance to my apartment, so I didn't worry too much about that. I also had a car that I could park in the back of the parking lot so no one would see me getting out of it.

You would think that John and I had nothing in common, but that wasn't the case. John may have been a white boy from, "the sip" as he used to say. He was majoring in finance, and even was a Republican, but he loved pretty women, to talk about politics, and sports. Growing up in the Springs, all politicians were Republicans, and I had a fair amount of experience with sports. At ASU, I was learning about politics. John knew a thing or two about both.

One day we happened to meet up at the same bar for happy hour, where we scarfed down all the free food we could stomach, while we sipped on beer that had grown warm. Somehow, we started talking about racism. I had experienced the "Snowcapped Rockies of Colorado" that Martin Luther King Jr. mentioned in his "I Have A Dream" speech, and I was sure I knew more about black people than he did. I didn't have a problem telling him either. To my surprise, John shot back and said, "Man, I grew up around more black people than you even know." He wasn't about to concede an inch about whether he knew more about black people than I did. John's confidence and apparent insight into African American culture caught me off guard. There I was, an African American having gone to all white schools, attending a predominately white university, and a white boy from Mississippi was telling me that he knew more about my own people than I did. It wasn't so much that he was right that bothered me, it was that he was smart and wasn't afraid to voice his opinion. Until then, most of the white boys that I knew didn't have the courage stand their ground, and have in an intellectual conversation with me about race.

John and I had fun too, lots of it. One night, we went to an upscale bar where they served jumbo-sized strawberry daiquiris. We were checking out the babes and drinking before I realized that John could hold his liquor too. We disagreed on so many subjects that we talked for hours, and drank for hours, and then John drove us home. On the way home, I realized that we didn't even talk to the ladies. John dropped me off, went to his efficiency apartment, and crashed as well. The next day, the only stories we had to tell were about how many fine babes there were in the bar and how we managed to leave the bar without talking to any of them.

When we talked politics, our discussions were legendary. John and I disagreed about every aspect of politics. He referred to himself as a fiscal conservative and social moderate. When I asked him if he voted for Ronald Reagan, and he said yes, I told him that a Republican was a Republican was a Republican. We argued about Reagan breaking the Air Traffic Controllers Union, putting small farmers out business in favor of corporate farmers, and making it more difficult for poor people to go to college. At the end of the day, politics was politics and people were people. John was good people.

The one thing we had had in common was sports. It didn't matter if we were talking about sports, playing sports, and watching sports, we had a good time doing it. Like my friend Herman, John was a good athlete as well. He was lifeguard at Dobson Ranch, an upscale housing community just outside of Tempe. He played pickup basketball with the best of us, played on a softball team, and skiied too. He wouldn't hesitate to throw around a football either. The one area where John and I couldn't find common ground, outside of politics, was with our women.

John was dating Janet, a redheaded bombshell, who was working at Circle K at the time. Every so often, I'd get a call from him, and he would say, "Brother, you gotta tell Boni to stop tellinig Janet that I I'm gonna dump her for a southern bell. Hell, every time I turn around, Janet's sweating me about leaving her." He was puzzled, and couldn't figure out why every time our girlfriends talked, they managed to end up talking about who was getting married and who was getting dumped. I told Boni several time to stop telling Janet that, but she didn't listen. That all changed when John married her. Now they have two beautiful daughters, a blond and red head, and son who looks like his dad.

MY FIRST LOVE

I didn't expect to fall in love with Bonnie. In Denver, Bonnie was a cheap date. We hadent' dated that long before I left for ASU. She stayed behind in Denver, continued to model, and legally changed her name to Boni Cherelle. Sure, we had fun together, but my plan was to leave the life that I knew in Colorado behind and begin anew in Arizona. As usual, God had other plans for me, and so did Boni.

When I arrived at ASU, I was single for the first 9 or 10 months, but my relationship with Boni never really ended. We lived in different states, and I was trying to leave my life in Denver behind. I had a rough life in Denver, and attending ASU gave me the best opportunity to begin anew.

I soon learned that Boni didn't plan on being left behind. When we talked on the phone, it was if she knew everything I did. She knew what color Speedos I wore to the swimming pool, how short my shorts were, that I wore sleeveless muscle shirts, everything. She also heard that Barry and I were running around dating rich white girls. I later learned that my sister Debbie, who was in law school at the time, was telling her everything.

When I called home to talk to my mom to see how she was doing, Boni was there. After I moved out of my mom's apartment, Boni moved in. Sometimes when I called home to talk to my mom, Boni answered the phone. I didn't mind talking to her once in a while, but I didn't like having to ask her to put my mom on the phone every time I called home. My mom and I always had a close relationship, and I called home every so often to see how she was doing. All the while I was attending ASU, Boni was planning to quit her job and move out to Tempe as well.

After my first semester at ASU, my sister Debbie and I rented an apartment together and she continued supplying Boni with information. In September, Boni shipped her belongings to Tempe and flew out. Now I had to tell the women that wanted to date me, that I had a live-in girlfriend.

Boni resumed her modeling career for a while before Debbie recruited her to attend law school. Boni applied, and was accepted, with a little help from my sister who sat on the selection committee. She enrolled in school the following year. By now, Debbie was a third year law student, Boni was a first year law student, and I was a sophomore pursuing my undergraduate degree.

My life had changed. Debbie and I had always been close, but now Boni was there and this was the first time in my life that I can remember being surrounding by a family that loved me. All of the arguing, fighting, and distrust that I had grown used to was gone.

Boni was adopted as a child, and lived with 10 or 11 foster families until her mom and dad adopted her around age 4. She had a younger sister growing up, who was also adopted, but they lived very different and separate lives. Now Debbie, Boni and I were all living together, in Tempe Arizona.

While Debbie and Boni were pursuing law degrees, I was trying to do the impossible, overcome learning disabilities, hearing problems, and fear of failing in my pursuit of earning an undergraduate degree. I realized that if I was ever going to escape poverty, my journey to a successful life was through education.

Debbie, Boni and I were all working on our college degrees, and expanded our social circles to include each other's friends. My friends, mostly guys, liked Debbie and Boni's friends, mostly women and vice versa. We all got along fine, and Boni was there to make sure that all the women I met knew that I was taken.

Until then, most of the women that I knew, including some of my sisters, had figured out how to use men to get what they wanted. They would use any means necessary to exploit any sign of male weakness or vulnerability. If you dared to share your willingness to delay immediate gratification, in favor of achieving future success, the women I knew would crush your plan, stomp on your dreams, and use all of their abilities to make sure that your self-esteem remained low and hopeless. Boni convinced me that it was ok to trust women, at least her.

It wasn't long before Debbie graduated and moved on with her life. Boni and I got married, and set about figuring out what we were going to do with the rest of our lives. During my senior year at ASU, I realized that God's plan for me wasn't all bad. He knew that I wanted to play football at ASU, and how hurt I was to have that plan snatched away from me in the blink of an eye. I was blessed that he allowed me go to ASU as a student, and to graduate. I was the second person in my family to earn a baccalaureate degree; not bad for the kid who struggled to read and right in Special Ed.

My journey through the streets of Denver and experiences at ASU had taught me a lot. But what did God have in store for me now? My sister Debbie graduated from the ASU College of Law, and my wife Boni was about to graduate from there as well. I wanted to be a lawyer too. As a lawyer, I reasoned, I could help black people who were denied justice, obtain it. I had learned all about the crimes that white society inflicted on black people in my African American Studies classes, so it made sense for me to help even the score. With a 2.3 GPA, my opportunities to attend law school were limited. I talked to my academic advisor and found out that ASU would support my participation in a Law School Aptitude Test (LSAT) prep course offered by Stanley Kaplan. I took the course and prepared to take the exam.

My financial situation was grave and I couldn't afford to pay the application fees necessary to even apply for graduate school. I ended up writing letters to all 13 of the schools that I applied for, and only one, LSU, declined to waive the fee. I applied to Harvard, the University of Pennsylvania and other prestigious colleges too. I had a somewhat interesting story, overcoming poverty, learning disability, and being struck by lightning. I also added my eventual success at ASU as further evidence that taking a flyer on me just might add to the diversity of their student bodies and that I could make it if given a chance. I received no offers.

SALT LAKE CITY AND CLEO

Both my sister Debbie and wife Boni, had participated in the Council on Legal Education Opportunity (CLEO) program and found it useful.

I got accepted into the CLEO program during the summer of 1988, and attended at the University of Utah, in Salt Lake City. There were about 30 to 40 of us in the program, mostly Hispanic, with few blacks.

At CLEO, we took three law school classes and received guidance from upperclassmen. The program lasted six weeks and I did the best I could. On the weekends, my friends Paul, Ed, David and I walked the streets of Salt Lake City looking for entertainment. There was none to be found. The alleys were swept clean and even the bums were clean-shaven. All the bars were dry and didn't sell alcohol. Instead, we did what other tourist do in Salt Lake City; we went to the Mormon temple to learn more about Mormonism.

We found that the founders of Salt Lake City believed that Joseph Smith was a prophet, ordained by Jesus Christ, to reestablish the church of God in our time. We also learned more about their tabernacle choir, and their genealogical beliefs of blessing their ancestors after death.

Mormons come across as nice people, but at the same time, many of them exhibited a deep-rooted dislike for blacks. While exploring the Mormon Temple, I learned that Mormons' believe that having black skin was the sign of a curse that God put on Cain for killing his brother Abel. I also learned that Mormons believe that Native Americans were evil people who slaughtered the "righteous" white people, who inhabited America before them. I was disturbed to learn about those beliefs because my dad told me that his grandmother was full blood Chickasaw Indian. There I was, studying law in a city where the majority of the inhabitants believed that I was a direct decedent of Cain in the Bible, and that because of that relation, I was cursed by God, and that even the Native American part of my heritage was evil. I couldn't wait to leave that state.

Racial issues aside, this was the door that God opened for me and I was determined to pass through it. I went to the University of Utah and participated in the program. I studied hard, made friends, and got to experience law school. My best subject was contracts, which surprised me because I wanted to be criminal defense attorney, not a corporate attorney.

On our final week in the program, we found Salt Lake's sub culture. There were private bars where you could even buy liquor, if you had an escort. We found out too late to enjoy any of it, but it was good to know that it existed.

As part of the CLEO program, they promised to help us get into law school somewhere. I was happy about that because my GPA was way below what was traditionally required to get into any law school anywhere in the country.

During my stay in Salt Lake, the University of Wyoming came recruiting. None of us knew anything about Wyoming, and the recruiter told us that Laramie was a suburb of Denver. Now I knew something about living in Denver, and recalled that Laramie was about two hours away. Nine of us decided to make the trip to Laramie, by car.

It was mid-July when we arrived in Laramie. It was sunny, the weather was mild, and the Law school faculty entertained us. They showed us around the school, the community, and held a bar-b-q for us. Their recruiting pitch was simple. They wanted to diversify their law school and invited us to apply.

Later that evening, we explored the nightlife in Laramie. We found the Cowboy Bar and the Buckhorn Bar open. We also found that Laramie had both kinds of music playing on the Radio, Country and Western. Then we remembered their recruiting pitch, that Laramie was a suburb of Denver. After a short discussion, four of us decided to make the trip.

My roommate Paul and I had both lived in Denver, and David had gone to school somewhere in Colorado. Ed was from New Mexico, and the four of us decided to make the road trip to Denver for the evening. We gassed up and hit the road. We actually had a good time in Denver, and drove back to Laramie early the next morning.

The next day, we decided that Laramie had something to offer, and we all preferred it to Salt Lake City. We met the Dean, who had actually spent time as an Associate Dean at ASU, and let him know that we were somewhat concerned because there were no second or third year blacks or Hispanics enrolled at UW. He understood and assured us that UW would continue to recruit other minorities after our class. We thanked our hosts, and told them that the four of us liked Laramie and were going to apply. They were delighted.

That Fall, I was admitted to attend Law School at the University of Wyoming. I was excited, but my wife Boni liked Phoenix and didn't want anything to do with Laramie. She had been working, part-time for a collections attorney, and liked the lifestyle that Phoenix provided. She had spent the last three years living in Tempe, liked the warm climate, and had made a few friends that she had grown attached to.

I had made some good friends at ASU too, but I wanted to become a lawyer like Boni and Debbie. It was clear that ASU was not going to accept me because my undergraduate GPA was too low. They also recognized that I wasn't one of those fearful Negroes who would stand by and watch as they trampled on our civil rights.

Many of the African Americans on campus looked up to me as someone who they could trust and turn to for guidance. This was a tough decision for me to make. My new wife didn't want to leave our friends in Phoenix, and Wyoming was my best option for Law School. I prayed, packed up my few belongings and moved to Wyoming, leaving my wife in Phoenix.

PART VI

VICTORY IN TOUGH TIMES

Chapter 10

The University of Wyoming and Graduate School

August, 1988, I boarded a jet plane at Sky Harbor International Airport in Phoenix, and landed in Laramie Wyoming aboard a propeller plane. I rented a car, and the drive into town took about ten minutes. Culture shock hit right away. I moved from a warm weather state to a cold weather state, and went from a university with over 40,000 students to a town of about 12,000. At ASU, you could meet people you liked and never see them again, and attend football games at Sun Devil Stadium that held over 70,000 fans. In Laramie, you couldn't go anywhere without seeing the same people over and over again, and the football stadium was small, and nearly empty for most games. But since graduate school in Laramie was the door that God opened for me, I moved into married student housing and planned to do my best.

I never expected to live in Wyoming for very long. But then again, God has a way of letting me know that following his plan might be different from my own. But in the end, I could expect his plan to better prepare me for the future that lie ahead. I took out another student loan, enrolled in school and bought my books. I also hooked up with my CLEO friends and got ready to experience life in Laramie.

That first year, Laramie was freezing. Law school was more challenging than I expected, and the culture shock of living in a small town set in. I made new friends, and formed study groups with my classmates. The first survival items on the menu were a heavier coat, gloves, a hat with a face mask, and boots. I bought a bike later. If you ever lived in Laramie, you know that the wind blows 24/7, and if you ride a bike, the wind blows in your face both going and coming.

As a former integrator of public schools, I was already race conscious, but in Laramie, I stood out like a fly in a bowl of cottage cheese. My Chicano brothers had a little more cover, because Laramie had a fair amount of Hispanics who lived in the community, and worked at the University. For me, the locals must have asked me a hundred times, what sport I played. Everyone was surprised to learn that I was a law student. How could they have guessed that? There were no second or third year African American law students.

My problems adjusting to life in a small town developed almost immediately. After a few weeks of doing almost nothing but studying, I went to a party and quickly learned what it meant to be a 6ft 2 inch black man in Laramie Wyoming. We all looked alike to the locals.

One day, I was at home studying when the Laramie Police knocked on my door. They wanted to question me about a crime committed by a black man. I knew that I hadn't committed any crimes in Laramie, but I fit the description. The experience was frightening. The officer invited me down to the courthouse to stand in a police lineup. I was new to the area, so surely no one could pick me out of a police lineup for a crime that I didn't commit, so I went.

When I got to the courthouse, I was the only black man dressed in a suit and a tie. The rest of the men wore blue jeans, t-shirts, and basketball shoes. One of the brothas, Oliver (God rest his soul), tried to strike up a conversation with me, but I wasn't interested. Here I was in a strange state, with no relatives to speak of, and standing in a police lineup. I gave him that, "You best be moving on" look that is usually reserved for criminals on the street, and he got the message. After the lineup, all but one of us got released. One brotha was returned to his jail cell and bound over for trial. I thought this brief brush with the law was over, but I was wrong. I soon got subpoenaed to appear in court. After the subpoena, the police lineup was no longer a bad joke. I had to take this seriously. While my friends and classmates focused on their studies, I worried about getting convicted for a crime that I didn't commit.

Later that semester, Boni drove from Tempe to Laramie and surprised me. I was surprised, and even shocked to see her; but it was a blessing that she was there. She provided moral support and helped me through the trial. I didn't know it at the time, but I found out at trial that the defense attorney had selected me as the person he wanted to use to help him establish reasonable doubt for his client. He wanted to suggest to the jury that I had committed the crime, not his client. When I went to trial, several months later, the judge sequestered me from the court proceedings, and I waited outside the courtroom while the trial got underway.

When I was sitting on the bench outside of the courtroom waiting for the defense counsel to call me as a witness, a clean cut, young man, sat down next to me and asked what I was doing at the trial. I told him that the police thought I stabbed a white dude with a screwdriver. The man told me that he was the white dude that got stabbed, and that he picked the guy that did it out of a police lineup. He assured me that I didn't even look like the guy. He went on to explain that he caught the defendant underneath his truck, taking a part off. He said that he told the guy to come out from underneath his truck, and when he did, the defendant took off running. He said he chased the thief and actually caught him, and the defendant stabbed him repeatedly with a screwdriver. He went on to describe the defendant as dark skinned, about 5ft 8 inches tall, with long, curly hair. By contrast, I was 6ft 2 inches tall, had light skin, with very short hair, almost bald. It wasn't until that moment that I breathed a sigh of relief. But, I still had to testify in court when the judge called me.

After about an hour and a half of courtroom proceedings and testimony, they called me into the courtroom and I was sworn in. The prosecutor allowed my wife to sit with the prosecution at the table as my representative. The defense council asked me my name for the record, and I told him. He was determined to get his client off and had been studying the case for some time. He knew all the intricate details of the case, and began his questions by asking where I was on the night of October 18 at 11:30 PM. I later learned that October 18 was the night of the crime, but I was a law student and the date didn't have any significance to me. I answered his question, "I don't know." The defense council appeared shocked, and asked me again, "Where were you on the night of October 18?" He reminded me that I was under oath had sworn to tell the truth. I answered again, "I don't know where I was on that night." The prosecutor objected to his repeating the same question and told the judge that the question had been "asked and answered." The judge agreed and asked the attorney if he had any other questions for me.

The defense council asked the judge if he could treat me as a hostile witness so that he could ask me leading questions. The prosecutor objected because I was the defense attorney's, witness. As a first year law student, I had learned that the defense usually called people to testify who supported their theory of the case. What the defense counsel really wanted was to ask me leading questions so that he could establish that I was in the neighborhood on the night of the crime.

The judge granted the defense councils request and he asked me if I had attended a party on the night of October 18. That date still didn't mean anything to me so I answered, "I don't know." The defense counsel looked frustrated by my answer and asked the judge to instruct me to answer his question. The prosecutor renewed his objection, and said that the question had been "asked and answered." The judge agreed with the prosecution and asked the defense counsel if he had any other questions for me.

The defense council, by now red faced, asked me, "Why don't you know where you were on the night of October 18?" I answered him and said, "I don't even know what day of the week October 18 is on." He got more frustrated and tried to find a calendar. When he couldn't find one, he said that he didn't have any other questions for me. The prosecutor had no questions and I was allowed to leave the courtroom.

The whole investigation and trial took several months. While my friends and fellow students were focusing on their studies, I was concerned that someone might say that I actually committed the crime, and that I would have to spend time in prison for a crime I didn't commit. I studied hard, stayed up late reading my law books, and wrote brief after brief so that I wouldn't get embarrassed when my professors called on me in class. I tried to focus on school, but every time I tried to focus on my studies, my mind kept drifting back to the trial, and the fact that someone in power wanted to blame me for a crime that I didn't commit.

That semester, I received two C's, two D's and an F. I was on academic probation, for the first time since my freshman year at ASU. The next semester, I received a B, two C's and two D's, and was suspended from school. I was devastated. I prayed to God. The next day, I made an appointment with the Dean, explained my concern regarding how the trial had negatively affected my ability to study, and asked him to reinstate me. He said no. By then, my wife had moved to Laramie and was studying for the Bar Exam, and I was out of school.

I made an appointment with the chair of the Political Science Department and expressed in interest in pursuing a Masters degree. My undergraduate degree from ASU was in Political Science and the department offered a Master of Arts in Political Science and a Masters degree in Public Administration. I applied for admission in the into the Master of Public Administration program, and was accepted.

That same year, my friend Herman applied and been accepted to attend law school at UW. He had taken a year off from college to figure out what he wanted to do with his life, and I talked him into coming to Wyoming. When he enrolled, he was shocked to learn that I had been kicked out of school for bad grades, but we were still friends and he encouraged me to continue with my masters and go back to law school later, if I wanted.

Herm was always a smooth talking ladies-man and soon hooked up with Linda, a Chicana sista, who was a few years younger than him. Linda had a bubbly personality, big hair, a coke bottle figure, and boy could she talk. If there was ever a lawyer locked up inside a person, it was locked up in Linda.

I had known Herm for six years by now and he seemed to really like this girl. He talked about her constantly. When I invited him to go to the gym, he had to talk to Linda. Out for a beer, talk to Linda. Play pool, Linda, Linda, Linda. I was already married and didn't have to talk to my wife that much. I almost couldn't believe my eyes, but my boy was falling in love.

We used to call Herm "The Last of the Mohicans" because I was married, John was married, Rob was committed, Smitty was married and even Barry got married. But Herm, he was untouchable. Now when we talked, he was saying all kinds of crazy things like, "Me and Linda are going to move to Alaska to practice law." I reminded him that we were already freezing our butts off in Laramie, and that Alaska was colder than this. I said, "Do you know where Alaska is and how long it would take to get there, even by plane, from anywhere?" He said, "Ya" and had this strange look on his face. I finally said, "Are you in love with Linda?" He smiled a sheepish smile, and said, "A little." Just then, I knew it was all over for my last bachelor friend from ASU.

Two years later, in May 1991, I completed my MPA and Herman and Linda had graduated from law school. I was looking for work and they were headed for Alaska. They did get married, opened up a law practice in Anchorage, and had two beautiful baby girls. I made the trip to Alaska for their wedding, and the flight was as long as I thought it was, even longer.

Boni passed the Wyoming Bar, and was working as a Staff Attorney at the university. She liked her job and the people she worked with. She was hoping to settle down, buy a house and start a family. Our problem was that happiness for me was seeing Laramie in my rearview mirror. I served my time in Laramie, and endured the harsh winters. I was tired of sticking out like a sore thumb. I wanted nothing more than to go to another state, any other state, except for Utah or Alaska, and look for work.

At my graduation commencement, as I walked across the stage as the only African American student to graduate with a master's degree from my college, the Provost, Dr. Al Carnig, stopped me on stage and asked what my plans were. I told him that I would be leaving Laramie soon looking for work, and he asked me to stop by his office the next week and talk with him. I did.

The Provost was a tall man, perhaps 6ft. 4 inches tall, and appeared to be of European, ethnic descent. He was a nice man, a brilliant scholar, and was launching a plan to diversify the campus community. At our meeting, he asked me, "What kind of work experience do you have?" I said, "As part of completing the requirements for my MPA, I did an internship in the Center for Academic Advising Center." He said, "Did you enjoy working there?" I said, "Sure" and told him that I enjoyed helping our students overcome barriers to achieving academic success.

In a matter of weeks, not months or years, the Provost created two new positions on campus. The first position was a Coordinator for Minority Student Recruitment, and the second was a Coordinator for Undergraduate Advisement. As things turned out, Oliver, who I had met in the police lineup, applied for and accepted the recruiting position and I applied for and accepted the academic advising position. Ollie and I agreed that if he got minorities to attend UW, I would see that they made academic progress and graduated.

Oliver was about 6ft. 1 inch, 210 lbs, and was from inner city Chicago. I found out later that he walked on the UW basketball team, and wound up being a member of one of the greatest basketball teams ever to play for UW. His team, led by Fennis Dembo, went to the Sweet Sixteen in the NCAA, Division 1 basketball tournament known as The Road to the Final Four. To be sure, Ollie was street smart, but he also managed to complete his BA at UW while playing basketball.

Ollie and I found ourselves working in Knight Hall. His office was on the first floor and mine was on the third floor. Our hires doubled the total number of African American professional staff working at UW from two to four. Like my friend Smitty, Ollie was a few years younger than me, but we got along fine. At first, Boni didn't like the fact that Ollie and I were becoming friends. Ollie was from Chicago and was known to have a hot head in the community. Boni thought that people might mistake me for him and vice versa. They did mistake me for him.

CENTER FOR ACADEMIC ADVISING

With my hopes of becoming a lawyer dashed, and a Masters in Public Administration degree in hand, I began my professional career as the Coordinator for Undergraduate Advisement in the Center for Academic Advising. My boss, the Director of the Center, was a nice man who was actually pleased that he got another person to work for him. He was glad because his boss, the Vice President of Student Affairs, was not able to grant him a new position.

Before I knew it, I was advising students, supervising graduate student advisers, and teaching American Government and Politics classes in the Political Science Department. I enjoyed advising students, and serving as a mentor to nearly 100 African American students on campus. I advised undeclared students or students who had not decided on a major course of study; international and national exchange students; and students who had to be readmitted to the university after flunking out of school.

I also advised a high percentage of African American students who sought me out because they thought I could relate to their experiences at UW. I actually had a lot in common with students that I advised, both black and white. Like many of my students, I was the first generation in my family to earn a Baccalaureate degree. I had to overcome poverty and all sorts of other barriers, including a learning disability and getting struck by lightning, to achieve the level of success that I enjoyed.

Most of my students were white, first generation college students who were a little apprehensive when they walked into my office for the first time and saw a black man sitting behind a large wooden desk. They relaxed when they found out that I was too was first generation, had graduated third from the bottom of my high school class, and that I even flunked out of community college. After taking a brief moment to break the ice, students I advised realized that they could trust my judgment and benefit from my advice.

I also supervised graduate student advisors. The Center employed two graduate student advisers to advise some of our students. We selected one graduate student advisor from the Psychology department and one from the Counselor Education department. All of our graduate student advisors were pursuing doctoral degrees.

One of our graduate student advisors that I supervised, Jay, was pursuing his doctoral degree in Clinical Psychology. He was almost 6ft tall, had blond hair and blue-eyes, and was from Minnesota. He told me that he came from a long line of Norwegians that settled in Minnesota. I believed him, besides, who would make up a story like that?

Like many of my other friends, Jay was smart. When we hired him, I saw his academic transcripts and he had all A's except for one B in some obscure course that I can't remember. He also liked sports, especially basketball and hockey. After I got to know Jay, I found out that he spent time in the Peace Corps, and was stationed in Africa. He told me all sorts of wild stories about his adventures in Africa, and how he managed to survive by drinking warm goats' milk, that he had to chew before he could swallow it.

He told about the time he was waiting for transportation through the bush, and he had to defend himself against a pack of chimpanzees, by picking up a stick, jumping up and down, and generally acting crazy. He was convinced that those monkeys posed a serious threat to him, and the way he retold the story, he had me laughing until I almost cried. Jay did his job well, and provided a welcoming atmosphere for our students.

Jay and I became friends and went hunting and fishing together, played pool, drank beer, and talked about all sorts of things including raising children. He always had good advice for me when I told him stories about my son Adrian. One day he came over to our house and saw Adrian run through the living room, jump on and then over the back of the sofa and keep going. Adrian was 9 months old at the time. Jay was in awe of his muscular body, speed and agility.

The interesting thing about Jay is that he completed his doctoral degree and married his girlfriend, Beth, who was studying to be a medical doctor. He eventually moved back to Minnesota, has two beautiful children, a son and a daughter, and is a stay-at-home dad. We still talk on the phone every once in a while, mostly about our kids and sports, and have remained friends. Occasionally we send a dollar back and forth if our favorite teams play each other. The looser has to send the same dollar back to the winner.

CAMPUS COMMUNITY

At UW, under the Provost's leadership, things were changing on campus. Along with diversifying the administrative staff, he also sought to diversify the faculty as well. To help achieve that aim, the Political Science department asked me to develop and teach a political science course for high achieving students. The Chair of the Political Department knew that I taught three discussion sections of about 25 students each, for a section of American Government and Politics. The introductory course enrolled about 150 students, and two graduate students split the load for discussion sections, teaching three each. I developed and taught the course, and the experience was extraordinary.

I selected a text that exposed my students to five perspectives of each topic under study, including liberal, conservative, radical left, radical right, and centrist or moderate points of view. I also taught the course using the Socratic method of teaching that is commonly used to teach law school classes across the country. Socrates, the famous Greek Philosopher, argued that learning must involve doing what one thinks is right, even in the face of universal opposition. According to Socrates, we need to pursue truth and knowledge, even when opposed.

What my students found most challenging about my use of the Socratic method of teaching was that it consisted of questioning them on the positions they asserted in class, and my exploring the practical applications of their thoughts and ideas through questions that revealed contradictions in their suppositions. This process proved to them that some of their original assertions often had several competing, and equally plausible possibilities. Like Socrates, I did my best to never take a position, so the critique of their thoughts and ideas did not come from me, but from their own colleagues' logical reasoning. Rather than sit through a boring lecture on government, my students listened to their classmates' opinions, because I might ask them to comment on their classmates' answers to my questions at any time.

For many of my students, I was the first African American teacher that they had ever had, and for some, I was the first black man that they had ever seen in the flesh. Many of my students were from small towns in Wyoming and considered Laramie to be the "big city." Some of my students were from towns like Sleepy Hollow, Wyoming, population 1000, while others were from as far away as New York City. Some of my students read the Northern Wyoming Daily News, while others read the Washington Post. Discussions were often lively. I exposed my students to each other's ideas and to ideas that challenged their own. For those who had done the reading, I also exposed them to well thought-out reasons that supported any of the five perspectives that they may have embraced as their own. By the end of the course, some of my students were surprised to learn that the author of the textbook considered their political views as radical, either to the left of liberal or to the right of conservative.

I also engaged my students in direct political action. In Wyoming, citizens can sponsor legislation and there are so few residents, that people often developed personal relationships with their representatives. In my class, students voted to influence the political process, rather than write a piece of legislation. They decided to organize a telethon aimed at getting selected state legislators to change their votes on whether or not to support a state holiday honoring Dr. Martin Luther King, Jr. For years, a majority of the Wyoming state legislature resisted establishing a state holiday honoring Dr. King. My class provided a safe forum for students to discuss a strategy, and provided them with the support they needed to implement their plan. The students used a phone on campus to make the calls.

One by one, the thirty students in my class spoke directly to the legislators who voted against the King Holiday. My students told them they were going to vote in the upcoming election, and if they didn't change their vote and support a holiday honoring Dr. King, that they were going to vote for their opponent and get five of their friends to vote for their opponent as well, and to hold on. They then passed the phone to the next student who made a similar statement, until all thirty of them spoke. Each of the legislators that my students targeted and called did the math, and changed their votes to support establishing a state holiday in honor of Dr. King. Wyoming was one of the last states in the country to do so.

The following year, the Provost took another step in his plan to strengthen the curriculum at UW. Until then, each of the colleges that made up UW determined what courses students had to take to get a degree from their college. The problem with that model was that business school students, for example, could focus primarily on business curriculum and not on reading, writing, critical thinking, or culture, at a time when society needed business leaders who could communicate better if they expected to compete in a global environment.

The Provost's plan also recognized that many of our students were under prepared for university-level curriculum because any student who graduated from a Wyoming high school could attend the university, without taking a college entrance exam. He established a committee and charged it with developing a course that would help, not only first generation students, but all students enhance their study skills, test-taking skills, time management, and introduce them to student support services. At UW, the Provost was a visionary leader with a plan, and not everybody liked his vision. Some people were afraid of change. They resisted his efforts and longed for the return of the status quo. They hoped in vain.

The Provost's plan called for a university-wide curriculum that any student who graduated from any of the colleges had to complete. All students were required to take three semesters of writing, three semesters of math, and two semesters of a science. They also had to take a global studies course, politics, creative arts and other courses. All UW graduates would receive a liberal arts education as part of their specialized degree programs, regardless of their college.

The Provost didn't stop there. He made academic advising a key part of faculty tenure and promotion. This move was bold and innovative because it helped transform the focus of the university from faculty centered to student centered. Now if faculty were absent during their posted office hours for advising, students could rate them low on their advisor evaluation that I helped develop as part of my new job. Low academic advising scores could potentially block tenure or promotion.

Change was in the air, campus was buzzing and the Provost was just getting warmed up. His evaluation of the curriculum at UW revealed that there were no courses where students could learn about African American history and culture. He provided the resources necessary for the University to start an African American Studies department. The Dean of the Arts and Sciences College conducted a national search, and hired the first graduate from Dr. Molefi Asanti's African American Studies department at Temple University, to chair the department. The new director was a large man, about 6ft 5 inches tall and 300 lbs, from Nigeria. Dr. Coker was a scholar who had accomplished much academically, at a young age. At UW, the prevailing wisdom among the white power brokers was that it was important for them to make sure that any people of color they hired had no animosity against whites. The new director was a Nigerian, and as far as they could tell, he had solid academic credentials and was a safe hire.

When the Director looked around for support to build his department, he found four African American professional staff on campus: Oliver; a female staffer who was a long time resident; a female counselor in the athletic department, and me. The director learned that I had taken a year of African American history at ASU, and that my Master's Thesis focused on the Afrocentric Paradigm to Organization Theory. He asked me to help him develop curriculum for the department, and to teach the Introduction to African American Studies course. The key theorist behind my Master's thesis was no other than Molefi Asanti, our new director's department Chair at Temple University. Dr. Asante sent me a signed copy of his book, "Kemet, Afrocentricity and Knowledge" and encouraged me to continue my pursuit of knowledge of African American history and culture. I accepted the directors' offer, and agreed to develop the course and teach it.

The Director did his best to build the department, but he soon learned what the African American community already knew, the VP of Student Affairs was more determined than ever to block any progress he had hoped to make. I think the director may have underestimated the influence and power that the VP had, but I had been to the Mormon Temple in Salt Lake City, and my boss was the Stake President. Mormons had built a powerful congregation in Wyoming, and it wouldn't surprise me if they took the state over sometime in the future.

God sent me to Salt Lake City, the national headquarters of the Mormon religion, and then surrounded me by people of the same faith in my first professional job. Good or bad, God exposed me to the Mormon faith before he arranged for me to work for them. As an outsider, unless you joined the Mormon Church, the network of people that the VP could draw upon to undermine your efforts was virtually invisible in the Cowboy State. In the end, our new director got frustrated and lashed out at the Provost, which I thought was a mistake. None of us, including the director would have had jobs at UW had it not been for the Provost.

FROM SPECIAL ED TO THE PH.D.

Following my second year on the job, I realized that there was virtually no growth potential on my job, and that I was wasting a benefit. The university would pay for me to take one course per semester, and I hadn't taken a course since completing my Masters degree. That evening, I went home and was talking to my friend Jason and he told me that his mother was a professor at UW, and that I should take a class from her. The next day, I stopped by Dr. Sherritt's office and expressed an interest in taking her class on Multicultural Adult Education.

Dr. Sherritt taught in the Adult Learning & Technology department at UW, and she welcomed me into her class. After taking one class, I was hooked. After the semester ended, I went to her office and asked how I could get into the program. She gave me all the paperwork and encouraged me to apply. I did, and the faculty accepted me into the doctoral program.

Once I was in the program, the pace of my life quickened. I was no longer bored, in a dead-end job, at a university that didn't value my existence, in a state that was so sparsely populated and overwhelmingly white that I began to get a complex. Now I was pursuing a doctoral degree, the highest credential in academia. The journey was anything but easy.

One night after class, I was driving one of my new classmates home from class when the timing belt on my 1987 Toyota Celica broke, right across the street from the Laramie Police Department. I went inside to call a tow truck to have my car towed to a service station, and to call my wife for a ride home. When I asked the clerk for a phone book, she told me they didn't have one for public use. The clerk almost seemed proud of herself to deny me assistance of any kind. I called home and asked my wife to pick me up. It was about 10:30 p.m. when I left the police station to wait outside for my wife. Laramie was so small that it would only take five or ten minute for her to pick me up.

As I waited outside of the police station, I noticed several police cars, lights on with no sirens, and traveling at very high rates of speed. I looked in several directions to see what the emergency was, when one of the cars sped up on the sidewalk in front of me. The second car sped up on the sidewalk behind me. The third and fourth cars pulled up directly on the street in front of me and screeched to a halt. They got out of their cars, pistols drawn and ordered me to put my hands where they could see them.

As it turned out, I was the emergency that night. The clerk in the police station had called the police on me. I raised my hands and assured the officers that there must be some kind of mistake. I explained that my car had broken down across the street, and I pointed at it, and that I had gone inside the police station to call a tow truck and to call my wife to pick me up. I showed the officers my driver license and my university ID. They put their revolvers back in their holsters and waited with me until my wife showed up to pick me up. Those police probably could have shot me dead and gotten away with it, and I think they would have, had I not remained calm and cooperated.

When my wife showed up in our Ford Explorer, and told them that she was an attorney, their attitudes changed. Now they wanted to be nice to me, especially after Boni asked for their names and badge numbers. We went home, glad that I had not been shot to death on the spot. Laramie had a history of hanging a black man from a light post downtown, and I didn't want to make history myself.

The next day, Boni called the chief of police and told him we wanted to talk to him about the incident that I had been involved in the night before. He agreed to meet with us. Boni also told him that we wanted to hear the dispatch tape that caused so many police to respond with their pistols drawn. He agreed to pull the tape and to have it ready. When we showed up for our meeting, the chief was apologetic. However, he had bad news for us. The dispatch tape had been reused, which we later learned violated their own policy. Therefore, he couldn't let us listen to the tape. We learned that their standard policy was to pull the tape and not to reuse it for one week. The dispatch on duty did neither, and no disciplinary action was forthcoming. In Laramie Wyoming, this was justice, take it or leave it.

OUR FRIENDS

My friendship with Ollie continued to develop and I learned that he was a genuine success story, straight out of the housing projects in Chicago. I had been to Chicago. My mom grew up near Jew Town on 1210 S. Sangamon.

My brother Rich and I had to go to Chicago on business, and I asked Ollie if he wanted to go. He did, and I bought us all tickets. We caught a flight in Denver and flew to Chicago. I rented a car and gave the keys to Ollie, and he made sure that we made it to our appointments on time. He also took us by the projects where he had grown up, and we got to meet his mom too. When we walked around the projects, you would have thought that Denzel Washington was visiting. Everyone knew Ollie, they called him "Main" and just wanted to be around him. My brother and I, dressed in suits, full-length cashmere overcoats, with Godfather style hats, looked like his bodyguards.

When Ollie introduced us to his mom, Rich was speechless. I was shocked too but tried to maintain my composure. Ollie's mom looked exactly like our mom, but a shade or two darker. Somehow, our moms had to be related. When Rich finally opened his mouth, he apologized for staring and told Ollie's mom that she looked just like our mom. Ollie couldn't believe it either until I took him to Colorado Springs to meet our mom. Then he realized what Rich and I knew, that somehow, our mom's were related.

We made other friends too. Jason and Denise were among our first friends. They lived in the same four-plex that we lived in after Boni and I moved out of married student housing. Our apartment was on the bottom floor and theirs on the top. We had a common entry and you could go upstairs to their apartment or downstairs to ours. I met Jason first, as one of my advisees. He was about 6ft tall, blond hair, type-A personality and loved sports, any kind of sport. Like many of my advisees, Jason was trying to find his way in life and just couldn't figure out what he wanted to do with his life. His mom was a Fulbright Scholar and was responsible for my pursuing a doctoral degree.

Denise, was smart, high energy too, and kept their home immaculately clean. Jason and Denise were the all-American couple. Denise worked for a furniture store and eventually became the manager. I wouldn't be surprised if she owned it by now. Every once in a while, Adrian would let himself out of our apartment and go upstairs and hang out with Jason. We didn't have to worry about what Jason was watching on T.V., you could bet that he was watching sports.

Niyi and Angie were also among our friends. They had three beautiful daughters and one of them was Adrian's age. Niyi and I worked together on several projects as he built the African American Studies program at the University. Niyi drove this little Lemans, and the seats had to go back to their farthest settings so that he could get in and out of it. He put a lot of miles on that car driving back and forth to the East coast.

Cliff and Genie were some of our closest friends. Both of them were university professors. Their daughter, Shira, was my daughter Maya's best friend for a while, even after we moved from Laramie to provide a more diverse community just outside of Denver to raise our children. Cliff was taller than me, about 6ft. 5 or so, and Genie was shorter, 5ft 5 or so.

My friend Ernie, a 5ft 5in Chicano brotha, kept each other company through our doctoral programs, collecting and analyzing data that we believed would shed some light on the challenges minorities in higher Ed faced. We also went hunting. I have to admit that Ernie was a better hunter than me, but Wyoming was his home and he was able to get us on private land to hunt. If I got skunked, he always came through with some meat.

FATHERHOOD AND FAMILY LIFE

By now, my wife Boni had given birth to our first child, a son, we named him Adrian. Boni and I went to all the Lamaze classes and were ready to be parents. I was ready to coach Boni, keep her breathing normally, and play my part in the delivery. The day Boni's water broke, we were in bed sleeping; it was about 4:30 a.m. We had her bag packed; I grabbed it, helped her into our car and drove to Ivinson Memorial Hospital. Boni checked into the hospital and her doctor checked how far apart her contractions were and how dilated she was, left the room and came back with another doctor. The second doctor also checked how dilated she was and told us that he didn't feel our son's head at the birth canal, but his rear-end. Adrian was breached and would have to be delivered by cesarean section. Our doctor scheduled the surgery for 9:00 a.m. and we waited in Boni's room. When the delivery time arrived, they wheeled Boni to the operation room. They allowed me in the operation room during the surgery, and I scrubbed up. I was glad that I had gone to all of those Lamaze classes, because I needed to remember to breath.

I watched the doctor numb Boni from the waist down, cut her belly open, and roll her skin back. Then I saw my son for the first time. He was purple, had his umbilical cord wrapped around his neck, and had a head full of curly hair. After the doctor removed the umbilical cord from Adrian's neck, he let me cut the cord and wash him. I left Boni on the operating table and accompanied the nurse to weigh and measure the length of my son. He was perfect, and beautiful, and I wanted to make sure that he stayed that way.

Boni later told me that she noticed that after she gave birth, I just left her lying there on the operating table and disappeared with our son. She was right. But when the nurse brought Adrian back to her, to hold and to nurse, I assured her that this was the same baby that she carried for nine months and gave birth to. No accidental switch-a-roo, Adrian was ours, and I didn't leave the hospital until I had a photo of him and a copy of his feet prints. I know every parent wants to brag about his or her newborn child, but my son was the handsomest child in the hospital nursery, and I still have his first day of life baby picture to prove it.

When Boni came home from the hospital, she took as much leave as she could to stay home with Adrian. I was so excited, that I could hardly work. We had a son and that changed everything. We did our best to childproof our home and adjusted our lifestyles to include caring for a child. We were happy to do it.

A few years passed and Boni gave birth to our daughter Maya. Because Adrian was born by cesarean section, we scheduled Maya's birth and went to the hospital on the designated date and time. I got to watch again and was a little less nervous this time. The surgery went according to plan and our beautiful daughter was born. I took the same precautions to make sure that they didn't accidentally give us the wrong baby. Maya was perfect and had a head full of curly hair. She was the prettiest baby in the nursery.

At the hospital, it was kind of funny that both of my children were born with heads full of hair and were so light skinned that they were almost white. By contrast, the white babies in the nursery were all bald, and pink in color. All of our friends, and the friends of those families who also had newborns in the nursery, were surprised when I went and picked up my babies. Neither of them had gone through the birth canal and had perfectly shaped heads, no bruises on their skin, and had lighter complexions than the white babies had. They were the best looking babies in the nursery.

Boni and I were determined to raise our children in a loving home and to make sure that they were well cared for as infants. We both worked full-time jobs so that we could afford to live the middle class lifestyle that we wanted. I learned later on in life that Boni wanted to live more of an upper-middle class lifestyle, but that's another story. We looked at all the childcare centers in Laramie and decided to go with a private daycare provider, Iris's House.

Iris's House was a large, Victorian style house, run by a nice lady named Iris. Iris took no more than eight children at a time and provided the home-style of daycare that we wanted. Her day care was two blocks away from the university, which was convenient for drop-off and pick-up. We grew to love Iris and her husband Smiley, who was a professor on campus.

EXTENDED FAMILY AND THE CASEY
FAMILY FOSTER PARENT PROGRAM

Nineteen ninety-four, by now I had the perfect family, a loving wife, a two year-old son, and a new baby daughter. Life was going well and we even managed to take a vacation every now and then. The year before, I recruited my older brother Clarence to continue his education at UW and he enrolled and was taking classes to complete his degree in Sociology. He, along with all of my older brothers and sisters, had dropped out of college without finishing. My friend Ollie got Clarence admitted, which wasn't difficult because Clarence was a good student at CU Boulder. He had received A's and B's in Chemistry and Physics, but dropped out of school after he fell ill to a chemical imbalance in his brain. Clarence had been hospitalized a few times after he went off his medication, but he came to Laramie and got stabilized on his medication.

Soon thereafter, Clarence approached me and Boni about getting his son Terrance, who he fathered out of wedlock. He was concerned about Terrance's welfare and wanted to raise him himself. Boni was an attorney, who was always concerned about the welfare of children, and advised Clarence on how to get custody of his son.

After Clarence arranged to pick up his son, I drove him to Denver where Terrance's mom lived. Terrance's mom had several children, most of who were being raised by their fathers, and my brother wanted no less for his son. We arrived at her apartment, and she had Terrance and his belongings ready. It was a courageous thing my brother did. He wasn't about to make his life better, and not do all he could for his own son. We loaded Terrance up and hit the road back to Laramie. We were all family and Boni and I did what we could to help Clarence and Terrance get started.

Ollie and his longtime girlfriend Sandy also had a baby boy, Ryan, who was a year younger than Adrian. Sandy was fine, straight up. She was about 5ft 5, bleached blond hair and looked like a white girl. She acted like a sista, and I really couldn't tell you what her ethnic background is. She was smart too, but like John's wife Janet, hadn't gotten a college a degree yet. We liked her, she was fun to be around and we couldn't figure out why Ollie didn't marry her. Eventually, he did.

The final piece of our family, at least for a short time, was our foster daughter, Rachel. Boni wanted to raise a foster child, as well as our own children. We joined the Casey Family foster care system and went through foster parent training. We enjoyed the training and it actually helped us develop some ideas on how to raise our own children. After we completed the training, we provided respite care for other families who were Casey Foster Parents. We attended the Casey events and thought we were ready to give foster parenting a try.

Our first foster daughter, Rachel, was twelve at the time and was the daughter of a white woman and black man. Her father was in prison and her mother remarried and had to choose between her biracial daughter and life with her white husband and the child she had with him. A key part of the Casey program was that children had to maintain a relationship with their biological parents. Once a month, we had to let Rachel go home to spend time with her mom and step-dad. Her mom confirmed what we had grown to believe, and that was, her new husband was a racial bigot and would never accept Rachel into their family.

Every time Rachel went home, she came back with all sorts of psychological traumas, and exhibited behavior that basically undid the trust and sense of family that we worked hard to build. Determined to raise Rachel as part of our family, we got her into UW Prep, which is where our kids attended preschool. Prep was generally considered the best education available in Laramie. She made friends and did her best to adjust, but she struggled to follow the rules that Casey and my family set for her.

One day after school, she was supposed to wait for me to pick her up and I got a report that she had taken off with one of her friends and two boys. Laramie was so small, that it only took me a few minutes to find them. When I found them, Rachel and the boys were trying to put their pants back on, but I think I got there before anything happened. They all lied their butts off, even in the face of getting caught with their pants down, but at twelve years-old, what else could we expect? I took her home and gave her time alone in her room to think about what she had done.

It wasn't long before I completed all the coursework for my doctoral degree, and Boni and I discussed raising our children in a more diverse community. We knew many of the African American children in the community, and several of them struggled with racial identity. There were so few African Americans in positions of authority, that many of the African American and biracial children struggled to develop positive self-images and became invisible when their "friends" insulted their heritage or told off-color jokes in their presence. I had grown up in a white community and wanted my children to attend schools that valued their diversity instead of looking at them as oddities with no cultural heritage worth studying.

PART VII

ATONEMENT AND THE MILLION MAN MARCH

CHAPTER 11

ATONEMENT

By 1995, Boni and I had a son and a daughter, and worked to provide a living for our family of four. I continued to advise and mentor students in the Center for Academic Advising and teach in the African American Studies Department. I also completed all the coursework for my doctoral degree, and begun the research necessary to write my dissertation. My research interest was on learning as a process of transformational change, specifically regarding African American men. The more research I did in preparation for the literature review for my doctoral dissertation, the more I learned how few studies there were that sought to explain how African American men learned. The research I did find showed a disturbing trend that suggested that African American men were more likely to be educated in prison than on college campuses across America.

It wasn't that long ago when my life of poverty, abuse and despair led me to commit crimes to stave-off starvation or to experiment with drugs and consume alcohol to escape the pain that my youthful mind was not able to absorb. I even went to the extreme in athletic competition preparation, and dedicated my life to bringing pain to anyone who dared to achieve a level of success that challenged my own success on field of play. God spared my life several times, and sheltered me when I made mistake after mistake on my journey through life. I prayed to God for forgiveness many times during my life, but now it was time for me to Atone for my past, antisocial behavior, and to stand side by side with other African American men, and reach out to men who understood the anointing that God placed on my life.

In order for me to become the man that God wanted me to become, and the man that I wanted to become, I had to challenge myself to improve my behavior, my thoughts, and action before I could challenge society to change the way it treated men like me, and in a more visceral way, get the society in which I lived to stop punishing African American men and even boys. I had to cross that imaginary line in my mind that emphasized our differences as Americans, rather than focus on our similarities. I had to have the courage to accept the responsibility for my own actions. My journey through Atonement, Reconciliation, and Responsibility took more inner strength and courage than I needed to walk among men who could end my life in a split second.

My atonement journey was a spiritual journey that allowed me to accept responsibility for the wrongs that I had done to other people. I underwent a critical reflection process, and made amends for my social action that God will one day judge. I learned humility, in the spiritual sense. I had to confront errors in judgment, in the presence of God, before I could begin the journey to correct them. I also had to recognize and honor those who went before me, some of whom paid with their lives, so that I could benefit from their struggle. It was on this journey, where I learned to become human, not merely an African or an American, and where I learned what it meant to choose to do what is right, even if that meant doing it alone.

As part of my atonement journey, I reconciled my social action with my family, friends and yes, my enemies to bring harmony into my life and to repair my relationship with God. I sought creative ways to settle long-standing disputes, overcome conflicts in my personal and professional relationships, and set aside personal grudges that were doing more to stunt my spiritual growth than anything else. To achieve this level of reconciliation, I had to first find the good within myself and then search for the good in other people, even people who despised my very existence. Once I found the good, I had to embrace it, build on it, and bear witness to it. Only by exposing my inner, most personal conflicts, could I reconcile my differences with other human beings, and stand together with friends and enemies to help solve our common problems.

The third leg of my atonement journey is personal responsibility. I had to take responsibility for my own actions, for my relationships within my own family, and in the communities where I lived. I am convinced that education freed my mind, and enabled me to dream impossible dreams.

However, I am more convinced now, then ever, that it will take the most talented among us to help craft a plan that includes recognizing our collective contributions to help America forge a more perfect union. I understand that my sacrifice must be joined by other individual sacrifices, and that by standing together, taking responsibility for our own actions; we can illuminate the path towards more meaningful and prosperous lives. Through my individual actions, and the actions of others, we must seek justice, show compassion for the sick, homeless, and those who have lost hope in human kind, and become the truth tellers to the world. Only then can I expect to receive recognition in the kingdom of God for my other worthwhile deeds.

THE 1995 MILLION MAN MARCH ON WASHINGTON

The 1995 Million Man March on Washington (the March) provided me with an excellent opportunity to stand side-by-side with my fellow man and strive to be a better person. Minister Louis Farrakhan, the leader of the Nation of Islam, put out a call to African American men to meet in Washington, DC on October 16, 1995 for a Day of Atonement and Reconciliation. The news media responded so negatively to Minister Farrakhan's call, that I was personally offended by their effort to discourage men like me from attending. Regardless of the stigma the media attached to Minister Farrakhan and his rhetoric, millions of African American men needed to attend the March. I needed to attend, and I did.

From the beginning, I knew that I was going to the March. Rich went with me, as a birthday gift. A few years earlier, Debbie launched the idea for the birthday club. All of my brothers and sisters, including me and our mom, put money in the pot to buy a special birthday gift for the family member that turned forty years old, fifty for some of my older brother and sisters. That year, Rich turned forty, and his gift was an all expense paid trip to the March.

Rich and I had committed a whole multitude of sins in our youth, but now we were husbands and fathers, and had left the world of crime and immorality behind. By now, you know that I am not a Muslim, and have a personal relationship with God. But it was clear to me from the beginning that nothing the media said or did, was going to keep me from attending the March. I suspect that all two million of us had our reasons for going to the March, but I went to build relationships with men like me who struggled to make our communities better places to live. I was doing my best to be a good husband and father, and if black men were going to March on the capital of the most powerful country in the world to Atone for our past behavior, I was going to be among them.

What people in America didn't seem to understand about the March was that God knew that Minister Farrakhan was the only African American man in the country who had the moral authority to put out the call. I don't believe that African American men would have responded to any of the other black leaders, including the Reverend Jesse Jackson or General Colon Powell. In fact, Reverend Jackson didn't support the March until it was clear that we were going to the March whether he supported it or not.

General Colin Powell, the black man who many believe could have become the first black president, spoke out against the March as well, and wished that someone other than Minister Farrakhan had come up with the idea for the March. The fact of the matter is that God has his own agenda. Nothing against Reverend Jackson or General Powell, I am sure that they are both fine men who contributed more than most to influence the trajectory our nation, but God knew what he was doing when he placed the call to march through one of the most vilified black leaders of our time. God has a way of making the impossible, possible, and uses ways that are in stark contrast to the conventional wisdom of man.

Because of my relationship with God, it didn't surprise me that God brought the idea of the March through Minister Farrakhan. When you think about it, God has a history of bringing about change, and he always does it his way regardless of what men think or say.

In 1 Corinthians Chapter 1 verses 26-29, the message is clear:

> For consider your calling, brethren, that there were not many wise according to the flesh, not many noble; but God had chosen the foolish things of the word to shame the wise, and God had chosen the weak things of the world to shame the things which are strong, and the base things of the world and the despised, God has chosen, the things that are not, that He might nullify the things that are, that no man should boast before God.

The overwhelming majority of black men who supported the March were Christians, not Muslims. Few if any of the pundits on TV, black, white, women, men, seemed to understand that black men refused to accept the idea that we were nothing more than criminals, athletes or entertainers. It appeared to me that the pundits were reading their own press clippings. They assumed that because they controlled the media, they also controlled our minds and our actions. Perhaps one of the greatest African American thinkers of our time, Carter G. Woodson, influenced them. Woodson wrote, "When you control a man's thinking, you do not to have to worry about his actions." With all of the mis-education taking place in America, black men are as free as any other race of men to think for ourselves.

Without question, the media has a powerful influence over what most Americans think. On the other hand, my life has shown me that education and experiential knowledge are also powerful tools that combine to influence our thinking. African American men marched in the spirit of Atonement to prove to ourselves, and to the world, that the media does not control our minds, or our actions. I am amazed that the leaders of the free world fail to recognize the glory and power of God. God does not have to seek man's permission to use the despised Minister Farrakhan, and two million African American men, to bring world-wide attention to the plight of the black family in America.

God blessed our trip to the March. On the way to the March, Rich and I flew from Denver with a connecting flight in Chicago. In Chicago, we thought we had a two-hour layover, not realizing that there was a one-hour time zone change, and we missed our flight to the March. So we thought. We went to the ticket counter and I asked the sista who was directing travelers to other gates for assistance. She said, "Where are you heading?" I said, "Were on our way to the Million Man March in Washington, DC." She said, "Take a seat right there for a minute." We did. She handled other passengers who were in line behind us.

When she called us back to the counter, she had booked us on a flight leaving in fifteen minutes. That sista didn't know us from Adam, and asked for nothing from us in return. She just helped two brothers who she didn't even know get to the March, on time. We thanked her for getting us on another flight, but didn't know that our seats were in the first class section of the plain until they called our seat numbers, and we boarded the plane. If that sista who shared a blessing with us gets a chance to read this book,

I want her to know that we appreciated what she did to help us on our journey, and that I have prayed for God to rain blessings down upon her. This was the first time that I flew first class. God blessed the March, and us too for going.

On board the plane, we watched as row after row of black men took their seats. In first class, there were eight travelers, and six of us were black men. We reclined in our soft leather seats, had a couple of free cocktails that would have cost us money in coach class, and talked about making history. During the flight, I raised my glass and said, "Here's to your birthday." We touched glasses and reminisced about the time we spent living together on Welton Street in Denver, the fights we had with each other and others, and how far we came as husbands and fathers. Surely if anyone needed to atone, it was us, and Rich said, "Thanks Dave. I need to atone more than you." I said, "You know that's right." We laughed and talked all the way to DC.

When we arrived at Reagan National Airport in Washington, our sister Debbie met us at the airport. She was no longer the little sister that we had to protect. She had grown to 5ft. 10 inches, had long hair that she wore twisted, and looked like a fashion model. We hugged and told her about missing our connecting flight, and how the sista at the ticket counter hooked us up with first class seats.

Debbie was living and working in DC as an attorney for the U.S. Department of Justice. She was the first person in our family to graduate from college, the first to get a graduate degree, and the first person to get a Masters degree. She may have been the youngest member of our family, but she led the way to success in higher education in our family. Debbie succeeded where our older brothers and sisters, including me, had failed. We stayed at her home in Southwest Washington, DC, that night. We had dinner and talked. There was much to talk about.

The next day, we took the city bus from Debbie's home to the Mall. When we arrived, it was electric. I took my VCR recorder and a 35 mm camera to record the day's events. As we walked around the mall, we met thousands of men, just like us, who were there to prove to the world that all black men are not the violent thugs, absentee fathers, or buffoons that we are often portrayed to be in the media. I wanted to show the world that African American men were hardworking people with jobs; that we love our women and our wives; and that we do our best to take care of our children. I also wanted to let our so-called leaders of the black race, many of whom encouraged us to reject Minister Farrakhan's call, know that in democratic societies, they have to bend to the will of the people and not the other way around. I hoped to help create a consciousness shift around how the world perceives African American men, versus the reality of how we as black men see ourselves.

As we walked around the mall, the crowd swelled, and swelled, and swelled. I climbed up in a tree and took pictures. As far as the eye could see, there were black men. For two city blocks, on both sides of the mall, there were black men. We stretched from the capital, past the Washington Monument, and passed the Lincoln Monument. Black men had come from every part of the country and some even came from as far away as Africa, to support our cause.

Debora Caruth and Richard Caruth, October 16,
1995, at the Million Man March on Washington

We walked past an ABC news crew, the reporter stopped me and said, "What's your name, where are you from and why did you come to the March?" I said, "My name is David Caruth and I came from Wyoming." I didn't get a chance to say why I came to the March because the men standing around who witnessed my response, clapped and cheered for a minute or two until one of them said, "Now I know that brothas came from every state in the nation, even a brotha from Wyoming came."

As we walked around meeting people, I asked the men I met the same questions that the news reporter asked me. I even asked the one white man that I ran across, "why did you come to the March?" He said, "there is no way that African American men are going to Atone for the wrongs that you have committed and leave white men out. White men have committed far more egregious sins against humanity than black men, and I am here to atone for myself and to support black men." I would give his name here, but when I listened to the tape of the March, it was so loud that I couldn't hear a word he said into the camera. The strange thing about not being able to hear the white dude, was that I remember the March as being the second most peaceful day that I ever spent on earth, with the first being my death at the time I got struck by lightning. Walking among my brothers, I felt safe, at ease and calm. We talked in normal tones of voice, told stories about our journeys to the March, shook hands and hugged. We shared food, bottled water and space to rest. I was surprised to view my video tape and not be able to hear the white man said who stood two feet in front of me.

The March was magnificent. Minister Farrakhan called for the March, black men responded to the call and made it happen. Sure, there were dignitaries and youth who made powerful speeches, but at the end of the day, the true blessing of the March was among the men ourselves. I felt the spirit of God among us. God is love and I felt more brotherly love at the March than I have at any other event in my life. We, black men, were the March and we responded to the call for Atonement. In the process, we created one of the greatest testaments of God in the history of the United States of America.

That evening, we left the mall and had dinner at Phillips, an all you can eat seafood restaurant on the Southwest Waterfront. We paid, took our seats, and went to the buffet. Phillips had an unusually positive feel about it that day. Literally hundreds of black men packed the place, big brothers like my brother and I, and we were hungry. I guess we were all hungry, because we ate all the food in the restaurant. The cooks emptied their freezers and the servers brought out all the food. We ate the seafood, pasta, bread, and the frozen yogurt. When we left, all they had left to serve was crawfish and we joked that some of the workers were fishing them out of the Potomac River. As we walked home, we passed by a housing project and saw dozens of black people who were oblivious to the March and were going about their nightly routines. It was a sad sight, but millions of us had taken a pledge to help those less fortunate, and we did.

FIGHTING BACK AFTER THE MARCH

That same year, my friend O'Leary and I started Caruth-O'Leary Research Institute (CORI) as means to use our expertise to help people. Our venture never made it off the ground, so I invited Rich to serve as the Vice President. Our mission was to develop and offer programs for the poor in our community by providing grant writing, program development and program evaluation services. We collected a modest retainer for our grant writing services, because most grants that people submit don't get funded, but as grant writers, we still had to spend the time necessary to find an appropriate Request for Proposal, write it, and develop a program that would meet the needs of both the funder and the community.

Rich had started a couple of other business ventures and written a few grants that got awarded while he was working as a manager of a privately owned, section 8, multifamily housing project. By now, Rich had completed his BA degree in Communications from the University of Colorado in Colorado Springs, and was considering working on a Masters.

I had taken grant writing as part of my Master of Public Administration degree and worked on some grants at the University of Wyoming. I had also completed all the coursework for my doctoral degree in Adult Learning and Technology and had taken eighteen hours of research methods courses, where I learned to collect and analyze statistical data.

Together, we set out to do some good in our community. We knew all too well, that if we didn't use our talents and abilities to provide discipline-centered summertime activities for kids in our hometown, then they would most likely get involved with gangs, sell or use illegal drugs or engage in other forms of deviant behavior.

Rich had been working with Master Tiger George to develop a tae-kwon-do based program for disadvantaged youth in our community. We used that model and developed one of the most successful, Tae-kwon-do based, culture-change programs in the country, "Fighting Back." Our aim was to reduce drug abuse and gang related crime that was ravaging the youth in our community.

Our "Fighting Back" program addressed a child's need to be included, have some control over their inner self, and feel a sense of affection. We defined Inclusion as the human need to be recognized as participants in human interaction. Children want to make a difference in their social environment and have some say over what happens to them. We defined <u>Control</u> as the ability to exercise restraint or direction over your environment. If children feel there is no sense of control, they are less likely to attempt significant projects or to initiate positive interaction with others. They become spectators and not participants in life. Similarly, we defined <u>Affection</u> as seeking a sense of interpersonal warmth, of being liked or loved. Children need to feel a sense of affection in their home and in their social/learning environments, and look elsewhere when this need is not being met. Without Inclusion, Control and Affection, we hypothesized that many children joined gangs and committed crimes.

Our research into the behavior of disadvantaged youth revealed a void between the amount of control teens are willing to accept in their lives, and the amount of control parents are required to give. We found that gangs recognize our youths' expressed need to associate, and have their associations noted. The lack of expressed and wanted control also contributes to the problem. In gang life, there are stringent guidelines that control and govern all members, first by choice and then by force. Children willingly relinquished this supervisory aspect of control to the gang, thus filling the void their parents vacated. We designed the "Fighting Back" program to recognize this pattern of behavior, and fill the same void. CORI's program invited parents to regain control of their children in a gradual process that also interjected the self-control their children needed to make positive differences in their social environments.

Our Fighting Back program accepted youth from as young as four years old to eighteen years old. We accepted fifty kids into the program: twenty-five of which lived in the privately owned, section 8 housing projects that Rich managed, and twenty-five kids identified by the local middle school Principal as being the most problematic children in his school. Master Tiger George, retired U.S. Ranger, provided the Tae-kwon-do instruction to our kids.

Many community leaders, politicians and law enforcement personnel contributed to the success of our program. Colorado Lt. Governor, Joe Rogers, supported our program, as did Dr. CJ White, Chair of African American Studies at the Metropolitan State College of Denver, state Senator Marry Ellen Epps, and others lent us their support.

I met Joe Rogers at ASU when he was attending law school with my sister Debbie and my wife Boni. When Debbie was a third year law student, Joe was a second year, and Boni was a first year law student.

Joe and I got to know each other because I had a job at the law school videotaping the students in their moot court competitions. Joe was one of the most charismatic and articulate students that I taped. Now, he was the Lt. Governor of Colorado, and the highest ranked African American elected official in the country.

Year after year, we wrote grants to fund the program, collected and analyzed data to measure the effectiveness of the intervention, and monitored the crime statistics in the neighborhood. I analyzed data and submitted reports to the Multifamily housing division of the U.S. Department of Housing and Urban Development. Our business venture lasted for nearly 10 years and we helped as many disadvantaged children as we could.

My experience at the March brought me in contact with hundreds of African American men, from all backgrounds, who were just as concerned about the degradation of our communities as I was. At the March, we pledged to help our fellow Americans. The March represented our consciousness of the challenges that increasing racism, deterioration of the social and economic fabric of our communities, and the urgent need for a new generation of transformational and progressive leaders in our society as a whole and in our communities in particular.

We didn't wait for change to happen to us, we became the change. We relied on the power of our brains, connections in the community, and God to open the doors of hope for hundreds of children who needed us to care. We did more than care; we brought our collective talent to bear on the problems that our youth struggled to deal with every day. The "Fighting Back" program helped parents learn how to reconnect with their children, helped children develop the discipline necessary to make positive choices in their environment, and exposed children to positive role models in their community.

THE SEPARATION OF WORK AND RELIGION

On my job, my career hit a major snag. My boss stepped down as director and the V.P. of Student Affairs had to appoint an acting director while he conducted a search. In the Advising Center, he had two internal candidates to choose from, Robert and me, both of us were Coordinators in the office. I think he wanted to appoint Robert, but most of the people on campus knew that being a director usually required a Masters degree and experience on the job. Robert had experience and a BA in Theatre, while I had experience, a Masters degree in Public Administration, and had completed all the coursework for my doctoral degree.

The V.P. called both Robert and I into his office and told us that he was appointing both of us to serve as co-interim directors. His reasoning was that he couldn't decide which of us to appoint and wanted to see if we could work together. Most of my colleagues privately told me that the V.P. would never hire an African American to supervise white employees because he was Mormon. The V.P.'s decision was a solution looking for a problem. My colleague didn't meet the minimum qualifications necessary to apply for the position, and wasn't a candidate. With his BA in Theater, Robert wasn't even qualified to supervise our graduate student advisors. I applied for the position, and interviewed for it too.

While the search ran its course, Robert and I had to discuss every decision made in the office. When we disagreed, and we did often, Becky, the other Mormon working in the office, had access to the V.P. in social settings and told him that Robert and I were heard arguing in the office. That was all the V.P. needed to hear to justify his decision to pass over me as director, and he hired a white woman with no academic advising experience as our new director.

My new boss, Karla, was thrilled to become our new director. While she spent time learning what we did, Robert and I went back to our former positions and did our old jobs. He was pleased that I didn't get the position, and didn't have to supervise him. I got the envious task of training my new boss. I also made an appointment to talk with Jessie (God rest his soul), our Employment Practices Officer, and asked him to investigate the VP's hiring practice.

Jessie was Hispanic, about 5ft 5 inches tall and a long time resident. He dressed nice and wore a long, black leather coat and godfather-style hat. He also was a friend of my wife Boni's. On most occasions, when there was an employment practices dispute, Jessie sided with the administration, and my case was no different. The thing I liked about Jessie was that he wouldn't just tell you what you wanted to hear. He'd tell employees the truth, and in my case, that meant that under no circumstances would the VP reverse his decision. If I wanted to move forward, I could have a hearing; but Jessie reminded me that most of the hearing officers were loyal to the VP and would more than likely vote against me. At the end of the day, I could expect the VP to retaliate against me.

Most of the minorities on campus wanted Jessie to hold the VP's feet to the fire, but we hoped in vain. My only recourse was to exhaust all administrative remedies and then file a complaint with the Federal Equal Employment Opportunity Commission. Jessie also told me that there was a huge backlog of cases because the federal government wasn't interested in possessing these types of claims, but that he thought that I had a prima-facie case of discrimination and that the EEOC would issue me a letter to sue after they reviewed my case. He estimated that this whole process would take a year or more to complete, all the while, the VP would go about his business of making my life more miserable than he was already making it.

I was preparing to fight when the strangest thing happened. I boarded a plan and went to the Million Man March. My experience at the March changed me, and when I returned to Laramie, I didn't see the VP through the same eyes. I made an appointment with him, went by his office and told him the truth. I looked him in the eye and said, "We both know why you refused to hire the best-qualified person for the job." As he squirmed in his seat, I shared my experience in Salt Lake City with him, not in a confrontational sense, but in a spiritual sense. I said, "God created man in his own image, and would not condemn an entire race of people as the Book of Mormon suggests." Beads of sweat formed on his forehead as we spoke. He fidgeted with his pen, when I said, "all men have souls, and God will judge men who profess to judge other men in his name."

I shared with him a little about my personal background, that fact that I was a Special Ed student, integrated an elementary school, that I had been struck by lightning, and had a personal relationship with God. I also took a moment to share with him that I made a decision regarding my complaint against him. I said, "I could fight you," and his grey eyes grew large because he was a small man, up in age, and I was 6ft 2in and weighed 220 lbs. and was in the prime of my life. But I didn't mean to suggest that I would fight him in the physical sense. I said, "In the spiritual sense." He breathed a sigh of relief, if only for a brief moment. I said, "God will fight this battle for me, and I will win in the end. After I witnessed again the power of God's glory at the March, my time would be better spent helping those less fortunate than me." I let it go. It wasn't easy to let go, because I already filed my paperwork with the state and it was only a matter of time before they investigated my claim.

Part VIII

Passion of Hope

Chapter 12

Earning the Doctorate

Most people don't understand the steps required for completing a Ph.D. First, there is the academic coursework. Doctoral students have to successfully complete our academic coursework and become steeped in subject matter expertise. Secondly, there is a comprehensive examination on all of the academic coursework. Failing our comps usually means that doctoral students may not have mastered the skills necessary to earn passing grades and that our doctoral committees were not convinced that our cumulative understanding of the academic discipline was sufficient to move on to the third stage, or the research and writing of the doctoral dissertation proposal. Third, there is writing the doctoral dissertation proposal. After completing the academic coursework and passing the comprehensive exam, doctoral students usually know where the gaps or under researched areas are in our disciplines, and we write proposals that will bridge those gaps, thereby creating new knowledge in our academic disciplines. Fourth, there is researching and writing the dissertation. After the dissertation is written, it has to be defended, orally, in public. All of us who have undergone this process have stories to tell about our experiences. I am no exception.

After I completed my comps, Dr. Donna Amstutz, the chair of my dissertation committee, took a job in San Francisco. Donna was a brilliant scholar, affectionately known by us graduate students as Big Momma. She was a white, heavy-set woman, with a pleasant demeanor and terrific sense of humor. She mentored and advised the few minority students who were pursuing doctoral degrees in the Adult Learning and Technology department. She was also raising her biracial son in Laramie, and told me that she wanted him to experience a more diverse, culturally accepting community for his last year or so of high school. I understood her concern and made a similar decision for my own children.

Donna was the kind of person who went out of her way to make sure that doctoral students she advised got the same opportunity to present our research, and attend conferences as white students. It wasn't uncommon for her to use part of her own professional development money to help offset our cost of attending conferences, by electing to sleep in campus dormitories rather than higher priced hotel rooms. Donna did the little things that made life in Laramie more bearable for those of us who had trouble fitting in for one reason or another.

As part of my academic coursework, I piloted my dissertation proposal idea and planned to write my dissertation on Transformative Learning Theory based on the experiences of African American males who attended the 1995 Million Man March on Washington. When she left Laramie and the University, my dissertation committee fell apart. My new chair required me to write a new proposal, and rejected proposal after proposal after proposal. For two straight years, she rejected every proposal that I submitted. Beaten, but not defeated, I prayed to God.

In my mind, I couldn't figure out why God brought me from Special Ed to the pinnacle of higher education excellence only to let me walk away in failure. I accepted the idea that I was never going to be promoted in my job, and now I was preparing to live with the fact that I was not going to complete my doctoral dissertation.

The next week, I was depressed when I got a call from my former chair. Always good natured, with a bubbly personality, Donna asked me, "Guess what?" I was depressed, the Mormon's had beaten me and I forgave them. Now I was about to give up on my dream of completing my doctoral degree. I generally wasn't feeling it when I answered, "What?" Her first words were, "The University hired me back. I'm on my way back to Laramie." I dropped the phone and hung my head. I was down to my last ounce of faith, and God answered my prayer, again.

When Dr. Amstutz got back to Laramie, she helped me assemble a new committee, worked with me to narrow the focus of my proposal, and began guiding my work again. The interesting thing about God's answer to my prayer was that I still had to work in an environment where I was not wanted.

Boni and I made a decision that we wanted to raise our children in a more diverse community. We were both applying for Jobs, and Boni received an offer to become the Associate Director of Employment Practices for the Metropolitan State College of Denver, and we prepared to move. We reasoned that I could get a job in Denver, and that we would be fine.

As things turned out, three weeks after Boni received her job offer, I also received an offer from the University of Wisconsin to be their Director of Academic Advising. Boni encouraged me to take it so that I could leave Laramie with my head held high. I almost did, but I had two small children that needed me, and I believed that I could get a job in Denver.

AFRICAN AMERICAN STUDIES

In January 1999, I accepted a temporary faculty appointment in the African American Studies department at the Metropolitan State College of Denver (Metro). Metro is one of the largest, urban, public, baccalaureate degree granting colleges in the United States. Metro was an open admissions college, had a campus in downtown Denver, and was the most diverse college in the State. I settled into my office in the Rectory building, and began preparing to teach four classes per semester that included a mix of Introduction to African American Studies, American Government, and Black Politics.

After classes begun, I contacted Joe Rogers, who was the Lt. Governor of Colorado, and asked him to be a guest speaker to my Black Politics class. The Honorable Joe Rogers accepted, and took time out his busy schedule to talk to my class about real life issues that he faced as Lt. Governor. He engaged my students, many of whom voted for the other guy, and answered all of their questions. Lt. Governor Rogers may have been a Republican, but he never turned his back on the people who needed him to stand up and give voice to their concerns.

In addition to teaching classes, I also had access to a college library that enabled me to order books, scholarly articles, and doctoral dissertations that I needed to research and write my dissertation. I had good access to the men who shared their experiences at the March with me, and bore witness to their continued efforts to advance the goals of the March in their own communities. I went to their places of business, had lunch with them and even visited some of them at their homes. These men were busy everyday making the lives of the people in their communities better.

While at Metro, I conducted a comprehensive review of the literature, collected and analyzed data, wrote and submitted drafts of my doctoral dissertation to my new committee members. My committee read drafts, made comments and their recommendations guided my work. Sometimes I agreed with their comments, made changes, and improved my dissertation. Sometimes I disagreed with their comments, incorporated them into my work, and improved my dissertation. Finally, I finished writing and defended my research, in a public forum, and answered all of their questions as best I could. When I was done, I still had to make a few minor revisions to satisfy their standard of excellence, and I made them. In May 2000, I graduated. My mom was right; I could do it, with lots of help from people who cared about me including my family, Big Momma, teachers, friends and most importantly, my faith and belief in God.

PRIVATE SCHOOL FOR ADRIAN AND MAYA

Both Boni and I both attended public schools growing up. Boni attended largely African American schools in Seattle, Washington and I attended predominately white schools in Colorado Springs, Colorado. We both went on to earn college degrees, even graduate degrees, and wanted to provide our children with the best education that we could. My parents were convinced that education was our ticket out of poverty, and I wanted to make sure that my children experienced a positive learning environment, especially during their formative years. I also wanted to make sure that they would never experience the kind of racial trauma and abuse that I endured as a child.

When we moved from Laramie Wyoming to Denver Colorado, my half-sister Regina, allowed Boni and Maya to live with her and her husband Gary Jackson, while we looked for a new home. My son Adrian and I stayed in Laramie until we sold our old home. We sold our house and found one that we could afford in the Cherry Creek School District in Aurora, and bought it. Aurora was the most diverse city in the state of Colorado, and the Cherry Creek school district was considered to be the best school district in the Denver metropolitan area. We wanted the best for our children.

After we bought a home and moved to Aurora, we enrolled Adrian in our neighborhood school, for first grade. Since I had the more flexible schedule at the time, I took Adrian to school. Boni, who was working at the Metropolitan State College of Denver at the time, took Maya to work with her and enrolled Maya in the college day care center. What Boni and I soon learned was that the State of Colorado was undergoing a change in education policy, and the school districts were implementing standard based education. What resulted was a learning environment where teachers were teaching children to pass the Colorado Student Assessment Program (CSAP) exam, instead of teaching them to love learning.

Two weeks into the school year, I paid Adrian's teacher a visit to see how he was adjusting to his new learning environment. His new teacher was a white female, thin, medium length dirty-blond hair with a pointed nose. She was surprised that I stopped by, unannounced, and that I was concerned about his academic progress, but she took a moment to tell me that she disciplined Adrian a few times. Her comment struck me as unusual because Adrian was a quiet, studious and even serious minded child. I asked, "Why did you think it was necessary to discipline Adrian? What did he do?" She replied, "He is just so social." When I asked her when she noticed Adrian being social, she said, "During math, he just talks and talks and talks."

I asked Adrian if he talked during math and he said, "Yes, I finish my problems and help my friends figure out how to get the right answers." I asked his teacher if she could show me the assignments that she had given him and she showed me. It only took a second for me to see that the math she assigned him wasn't challenging him. When I told her this, she said, "Adrian hasn't demonstrated an aptitude for math." I smiled at the thought of her ignorance and replied, "Do you mind testing him anyway, just to be on the safe side?" Adrian's teacher tested him and was surprised to learn that he tested out of first grade math. To learn math at his new school, Adrian had to leave his peers during math, and go to the second grade math class.

Having chosen education as a career, I knew that the public education system was failing minority students at an alarming rate, and I wasn't about to allow what happened to me during my childhood, to happen to my son. That evening at the dinner table, we all talked about the day's events. Adrian and Maya shared what they learned at their schools, Maya in preschool and Adrian in first grade, before Boni shared her day at work and I shared mine. After Boni told us about her day, I shared my experience with Adrian's teacher and Boni and I started looking for a new school.

My half-sister Regina suggested that we look into Stanley British Primary School. She heard it was a good school, and had a friend who oversaw the admission process at the school. Boni made contact and we scheduled a visit to the school. Stanley's philosophy and campus impressed us. Stanley is a private school, located on a portion of what used to be Lowry Air Force Base in Denver. Carolyn Hambidge, Bea Romer (wife of former Colorado Governor Roy Romer) and others helped found the school. Boni and I were excited that diversity was an important part of the school mission and that the learning philosophy promoted an innovative approach to educating children. Stanley also had a multi-grade learning environment that allowed students who excelled in certain subjects to work at their own pace and remain in the same learning environment with their peers.

After Adrian and Maya enrolled at Stanley, I discovered that many of the teachers used a variation of Howard Gardner's' Multiple Theories of Intelligence approach to learning, which I believe allows teachers to honor each child's individual gifts. In my childhood, I took many beatings and suffered from low self-esteem because I was a slow reader, and my genius in math went unnoticed. I wanted to make sure that my children were free to learn at their own pace and that their individual talents were nurtured. I take my hat off to Mrs. Hambidge and Mrs. Romer for starting a school that put student learning first.

After a year at Stanley, I enjoyed the privilege of being elected to serve a three-year term as a parent representative on the Board of Trustees. I served many more years as an active member of the diversity committee. Both of my children enjoyed the learning environment at Stanley, actively participated in extracurricular activities, and volunteered their time to bring joy to the lives of the elderly in our community. They both learned how to play musical instruments. Adrian learned how to play the Saxophone and Maya learned how to play the Flute and Keyboard. Adrian also tried the Conga Drums, and both of them sang in the Colorado Children's Choir.

At Stanley, Adrian and Maya experienced a learning environment that recognized them as people first, and then for their individual talents. I talked to my kids, and as they matured and progressed from one grade to the next, they let me know when their challenges were a result of their behavior or unfair treatment. They learned to speak up for themselves and to accept responsibility for their actions. I guess time will tell if they developed positive self-images or if they have to overcome self-hatred that plagues a large segment of our society and often results in feelings of inadequacy and despair.

In addition to getting a good education, Adrian enjoyed playing sports. He played football, ran track, and excelled in basketball. He played high school basketball for Denver School of Science and Technology (DSST). He also got invited, along with 50 other talented athletes from across the country, to attend the P.L.A.Y. Academy in Mount Holyoke Massachusetts.

Adrian Caruth, right, shooting over unknown player at the P.L.A.Y. Academy. The Planned Learning Achievement for Youth Academy is a certified basketball camp under the National Collegiate Athletic Association (NCAA), 2009

Adrian graduated from DSST and went on to attend college at the University of Colorado at Boulder, and is majoring in Business.

At the same time, Maya also enjoyed participating in sports. While at Stanley, she played volleyball and basketball. However, what I notice most about Maya is her love for cooking. I was always first to eat the easy-bakeoven treats that she made, and I often supervised her cooking when she graduated to being able to use the real kitchen. She also enjoyed helping me when I bar-b-q'd. We talked about recipes, ingredients, and tasted food before it was served for dinner.

After Stanley, Maya also took up modeling and participated in the Colorado Junior Miss competition.

Maya Caruth at the Colorado Junior Miss
Pageant, Denver, Colorado, 2009.

Being a father is a blessing. Sometimes, dads have to make difficult decisions to provide our children with a loving home. I tried to keep my children from inheriting the mindset of poverty that I endured as a child. My passion of hope is that Adrian and Maya learn from my experiences and embrace the good in people. In the end, I hope that they realize that they too can achieve the impossible dream, if they are willing to establish a personal relationship with God, and recognize when miracles present themselves in their lives.

CONCLUSION

From the day I was born, God knew me. He saw a child who was born with physical and learning disabilities, into an impoverished, abusive, dysfunctional family that was struggling to make a way out of no way. He knew both of my parents' limitations and provided for us. We didn't always get enough to eat, but just as God provides for the birds in the sky, and the worms underground, he provided for our family. He also provided me with access to education, athletic competition, spiritual healing, and friendships.

One of the strangest and most unnerving aspects of getting struck by lightning is that I stood at the gate of heaven as my life flashed before my eyes, not just the first seventeen years, all of it. The best way to describe what I saw in the spiritual world can be found in Genesis 28:17. "How awesome is this place! This is none other than the house of God, and this is the gate of heaven!" On far too many occasions, I have felt that eerie déjà-vu feeling of living a life that I already lived. What is most troubling is that I now understand the intersection between my thoughts and action, and the spiritual world. I know that a mere thought is harmless; however, when thoughts are spoken, written, acted upon or communicated in some way to another person, that same thought can have an everlasting impact on our lives.

As spiritual beings, we have to be mindful about what we say or otherwise communicate to others. A mere thought, or idea can motivate us to act, and that action can set in motion a chain of events that can change the course of our lives, and enable us to receive or miss God's blessings.

In a spiritual sense, our thoughts and ideas affect our behavior and enable us to develop inner strength. This inner strength allows us to increase our faith in the power of God, especially when we feel most vulnerable and alone. At the same time, in the physical world, our thoughts and ideas can cause us to lose faith. Our loss of faith can lead to loss of inner strength, and we can experience a sense of hopelessness and despair. Feeling hopeless can create barriers that separate our spiritual being from God's will.

In the end, we all need to be able to recognize when God is working miracles in our lives. Sometimes the miracles are pleasant; however, sometimes they are tragic. Either way, we have to recognize them when they happen so that we can appreciate when God is providing us with opportunities to keep Him at the forefront of our thoughts and actions.

My mom told me the story about a man who walked with God all of his life and noticed one day that there was only one set of footprints in the sand. After he looked down and only saw one set of footprints in the sand, the man cried out "God where are you?" Hearing nothing, he cried out again, "God, why did you abandon me?" God replied to his humble servant, and said, "My son, you only see one set of footprints in the sand because that was when I was carrying you."

I don't know why or how God decides which people He uses to make his presence here on earth known to man. What I do know is that I have felt His power. From the day that I got struck by lightning, I knew that my life was changed forever. I knew that I would have to share parts of my life with people that I would prefer remained secret. I also knew that I would resist putting pen to paper because I feared what people would think about me after learning that I committed crimes, behaved immorally, or learned about my struggle over life and death with God. How could I tell people who loved me that I chose death over life, three times, but God would not allow me to accept death? Instead, I had to live my life and battle through numerous obstacles so that I could fulfill God's promise to me.

With God in my life, I overcame the pain of being born into poverty with both a physical disability and dyslexia. I overcame being black and male in a society that is tilted so much in favor of the dominant culture that I would have a better chance of getting struck by lightning than I would overcoming my own limitations to achieve success. I felt the pain of racism, child abuse, mental abuse, parental divorce, physical injury, depression and despair. I escaped death so many times that I lost count and succeeded against seemingly insurmountable odds.

When I reflect upon my life, my greatest strength comes from understanding my mom's wisdom and establishing a relationship with God. My story should be a tragedy. It's not, it is a story of triumph over adversity, hope over hopelessness, courage over fear and above all else, it is a story of my learning to accept the power of God and recognize that miracles happen in our lives according to God's timing, not our own.

I am no longer afraid to admit that I blamed God for my shortcomings. However, I no longer do. I accept the shift in my relationship with God and reevaluated the choices I made in my life. What I have learned is that we don't have to be frightened by the idea that we have done things wrong. It is better to understand that God expects us to do wrong. In the end, we have no choice but to accept what we have done in the physical world. We have to learn how to forgive ourselves for the mistakes that we make and to forgive others without regret. Regrets are useless, so don't dwell on them. Instead, take what you have learned in this book, and throughout your life, and build on the positive things you have experienced. Realize that I did nothing, on my own to earn God's involvement in my life. I am humbled that He forgave my faults and chose to make me a Fisher of Men. For that, I am forever grateful.

REFERENCES

Caruth, D. (2000). African American Male Transformative Learning: An Afrocentric Study of the Million-Man March (Doctoral dissertation, University of Wyoming, 2000).

Sanders, B. (1988). The Caruths: Dallas' Landed Gentry. Dallas: Sanders Press.

Woodson, C. G. (1933). The Mis-Education of the Negro. Associated Publishers.